CHRISTIAN REFLECTIONS

CHRISTIAN REFLECTIONS

by
C. S. LEWIS

Edited by
WALTER HOOPER

WILLIAM B. EERDMANS PUBLISHING COMPANY
GRAND RAPIDS, MICHIGAN

Printed in the United States of America

CONTENTS

PREFACE

Shortly after his conversion in 1929, C. S. Lewis wrote to a friend: 'When all is said (and truly said) about the divisions of Christendom, there remains, by God's mercy, an enormous common ground.'[1] From that time on Lewis thought that the best service he could do for his unbelieving neighbours was to explain and defend the belief that has been common to nearly all Christians at all times—that 'enormous common ground' which he usually referred to as 'mere' Christianity.

He was a thoroughgoing supernaturalist, believing in the Creation, the Fall, the Incarnation, the Resurrection, the Second Coming, and the Four Last Things (death, Judgement, Heaven, Hell). His defence of 'mere' Christianity was colourfully varied, depending on which part of the line needed defending; to that part which seemed thinnest he naturally went, adapting his tactics to suit his audience. Such, I think, is evident from this rather heterogeneous collection of Christian 'Reflections'. These fourteen papers, which I have attempted to arrange chronologically, were composed over the last twenty-odd years of Lewis's life; some were written specifically for periodicals; others, published here for the first time, were read to societies in and around Oxford and Cambridge. There are passages in some of the earlier papers where readers will find anticipations of his later work; but such overlaps are inevitable.

There is not yet available any such thing as *The Complete Works of C. S. Lewis* which a person could buy in a set of uniform volumes. But if the *Works* were obtainable (almost all are easy to secure as separate books) and one were to read from start to finish all the volumes called 'Religious Writings' he would, I think, be struck by what I consider the central premise of all Lewis's theological works—a premise implicit, even, in his books on other subjects. It is that *all* men are immortal.

I think this deserves singular emphasis; not only because it is

[1] From an unpublished letter to Dom Bede Griffiths, O.S.B. (c. 1933).

vii

such an important ingredient in Lewis's understanding of 'mere' (i.e. 'pure') Christianity, but because the fact that men are immortal is news to many people today. And (a point in which Lewis would support me), because most of the modern liberal theologians are so busy being 'relevant' (or whatever else is in fashion) that they make no effective presentation of 'mere' Christianity—the Everlasting Gospel—to those for whom Christ died.

To illustrate this particular feature of orthodox Christianity which Lewis constantly underlined, one need only refer to the well-known *Screwtape Letters*. Lewis himself considered the book's popularity disproportionate to its worth: he liked *Perelandra* best of all his works and thought it worth twenty *Screwtapes*. Still though he bore a grudge against the book and chafed at having always to be 'the author of *The Screwtape Letters*' on the dust-jackets of most of his subsequent books, I never heard him say anything that could be taken as a retraction of its contents.

Screwtape's advice to his nephew, Wormwood, has been read by, and has edified (I expect), millions of readers. But, like many well-known books, it has its debunkers; most of whom debunk it for the same reason. One critic recently wrote: 'With the concentration camps across the Channel and the blitz at home, Screwtape seems to have been aiming at rather small targets and to have been decidedly lacking in the historical imagination ... Lewis was a better student of the daily scene than he often realized; but less equipped to venture beyond the flaming ramparts of the world.'[1] Another writer, attempting to 'disentangle what is of permanent value ... from what is ephemeral' in Lewis's works, notes the 'general moral pettiness' of *The Screwtape Letters*, adding that 'In the age which has produced Auschwitz, it is distasteful to have such slight topics associated with human damnation.'[2]

I dare say Lewis would have replied that damnation is far more likely to be distasteful than topics associated with it. But can anything which leads to damnation be 'petty'? Despite the fact that Auschwitz is an almost unparalleled instance of human wickedness and human suffering, it would have been an inappropriate example for Lewis's purpose. It is in one sense, the wrong *kind* of

[1] Graham Hough, 'The Screwtape Letters', *The Times* (10 Feb. 1966), p. 15.
[2] W. W. Robson, 'C. S. Lewis', *The Cambridge Quarterly*, vol. I (Summer, 1966), p. 253.

thing: its 'bigness', so to speak, and uniqueness blunt its usefulness as a universal temptation to sin. Lewis's answer to such critics—his answer to what *Screwtape* is about—is writ plain in Screwtape's caution to the younger devil:

You will say that these are very small sins; and doubtless like all young tempters, you are anxious to be able to report spectacular wickedness [Auschwitz?]. But do remember, the only thing that matters is the extent to which you separate the man from the Enemy. It does not matter how small the sins are provided that their cumulative effect is to edge the man away from the Light and out into the Nothing. Murder is no better than cards if cards can do the trick. Indeed the safest road to Hell is the gradual one—the gentle slope, soft underfoot, without sudden turnings, without milestones, without signposts.[1]

Because Lewis emphasized the reality of hell, not only in *Screwtape* but in *The Problem of Pain* (specially chapter VIII) and other books, it is often inferred that he was preoccupied with it— simply *wanted* it to be true. This indeed is to misunderstand not only Lewis but the Faith itself. For him the real problem was: so much mercy, yet *still* there is hell. Regardless of what we all wish Christianity were, he knew that this terrible doctrine has the support of Scripture (specially of Our Lord's own words) as well as that of reason: 'If a game is played, it must be possible to lose it.'[2]

I remember one very warm day when Lewis and I were reading in his study that I remarked, rather too loudly: 'Wheew! It's hot as hell!'—'How do *you* know?' came his answer. 'Better not say that.' I knew at once that he referred—more by the tone of his voice than anything else—to hell as the possible destination of some of us. The contemporary preoccupation with 'individual freedom' and 'rights' has deceived so many of us into imagining that we can make up our *own* theology, that Lewis's orthodox belief in a real heaven and hell strikes us as little short of fanatical: 'As there is one Face above all worlds merely to see which is irrevocable joy, so at the bottom of all worlds that face is waiting whose sight alone is the misery from which none who beholds it can recover. And though there [seem] to be, and indeed [are], a

[1] *The Screwtape Letters*, London: Geoffrey Bles Ltd. (1942), pp. 64–5.
[2] *The Problem of Pain*, London: Geoffrey Bles Ltd. (1940), p. 106.

thousand roads by which a man could walk through the world, there [is] not a single one which [does] not lead sooner or later either to the Beatific or the Miserific Vision.'[1]

It would not be enough to leave the matter here. From everything that I heard Lewis say, certainly from his writings, I know that the 'Face above all worlds' was to him the most concrete and desirable of all realities. But he never forgot that every human soul would enjoy ultimately a vision either Beatific or Miserific. In a passage from his sermon 'The Weight of Glory', beside which modern liberal theology seems embarrassingly vapid, he strikes at the heart of the matter:

It is a serious thing to live in a society of possible gods and goddesses, to remember that the dullest and most uninteresting person you talk to may one day be a creature which, if you saw it now, you would be strongly tempted to worship, or else a horror and a corruption such as you now meet, if at all, only in a nightmare. All day long we are, in some degree, helping each other to one or other of these destinations. It is in the light of these overwhelming possibilities, it is with the awe and the circumspection proper to them, that we should conduct all our dealings with one another, all friendships, all loves, all play, all politics. There are no *ordinary* people. You have never talked to a mere mortal. Nations, cultures, arts, civilizations—these are mortal, and their life is to ours as the life of a gnat. But it is immortals whom we joke with, work with, marry, snub, and exploit—immortal horrors or everlasting splendours. This does not mean that we are to be perpetually solemn. We must play. But our merriment must be of that kind (and it is, in fact, the merriest kind) which exists between people who have, from the outset, taken each other seriously—no flippancy, no superiority, no presumption. And our charity must be a real and costly love, with deep feeling for the sins in spite of which we love the sinner—no mere tolerance or indulgence which parodies love as flippancy parodies merriment. Next to the Blessed Sacrament itself, your neighbour is the holiest object presented to your senses. If he is your Christian neighbour he is holy in almost the same way, for in him also Christ *vere latitat*—the glorifier and the glorified, Glory Himself, is truly hidden.[2]

I trust that I shall not labour the emphasis Lewis placed on the *either-or* of the Christian faith by recording a couple of snatches from my conversation with him—primarily in order to

---

[1] *Perelandra*, London: The Bodley Head (1943), p. 126, (Tenses Altered).

[2] 'The Weight of Glory', *Theology*, vol. XLIII (Nov. 1941), pp. 273-74.

underline how solid this reality stood for him, not only in the pulpit or in the heat of writing, but in 'the light of common day'.

We were talking one time about a bore whom we both knew, a man who was generally recognized as being almost unbelievably dull. I told Lewis that the man succeeded in interesting me by the very intensity of his boredom. 'Yes' he said, 'but let us not forget that Our Lord might well have said "As ye have done it unto one of the least of these my bores, ye have done it unto me." ' There was a twinkle in his eye as he said it and we both laughed, yet knowing at the same time that it was no joke. On another occasion I mentioned that I knew of a man's grave, the epitaph on whose tombstone read 'Here lies an atheist, all dressed up but with nowhere to go.' Lewis replied: 'I bet he wishes that were so.'

I should now, before introducing the papers in this book, like to record to Lewis's credit a positive restraint which he put upon all his theological works. As he was minded to write only about 'mere' Christianity, so he steadfastly refused to write about *differences* of belief. He knew that discussions (or, more likely, arguments) about differences in doctrine or ritual were seldom edifying. At least, he considered it far too dangerous a luxury for himself—far better stick to that 'enormous common ground'.

He made no exception even in his conversation, a fact I know to my own shame. I remember the first (and only) time I mentioned 'low' and 'high' churchmanship in his presence. He looked at me as though I had offered him poison. 'We must *never* discuss that' he said, gently but firmly. Again, shortly before the publication of *Honest to God* in the United States, the editor of a popular American magazine asked Lewis to write a critique of the book for his columns. Lewis wrote back: What would you yourself think of me if I did? . . . A great deal of my utility has depended on my having kept out of dog-fights between professing schools of "Christian" thought. I'd sooner preserve that abstinence to the end.' This 'abstinence' has surely not weakened our conception of the Faith; his salutary single-mindedness has, rather, shown us its balance and true colours such as (I believe) few Christian apologists have succeeded in doing. Lewis, I think, understood very well what diet Our Lord intended when He commanded the Apostle '*Feed* my sheep.'

PREFACE

I am grateful to all those who have permitted me to reprint some of the papers in this book. (1) 'Christianity and Literature' was read to a religious society in Oxford and is reprinted from *Rehabilitations and Other Essays* (Oxford, 1939). (2) The three papers which I have collected under the title 'Christianity and Culture' include only Lewis's part in a controversy which first appeared in the columns of *Theology*. The entire controversy is composed of the following papers:

1. C. S. Lewis, 'Christianity and Culture', *Theology*, vol. XL (March 1940), pp. 166–79.
2. S. L. Bethell and E. F. Carritt, 'Christianity and Culture: Replies to Mr Lewis', *ib.*, vol. XL (May 1940), pp. 356–66.
3. C. S. Lewis, 'Christianity and Culture' (a letter), *ib.*, vol. XL (June 1940), pp. 475–77.
4. George Every, 'In Defence of Criticism', *ib.*, vol. XLI (Sept. 1940), pp. 159–65.
5. C. S. Lewis, 'Peace Proposals for Brother Every and Mr Bethell', *ib.*, vol. XLI (Dec. 1940), pp. 339–48.

I beg the reader to note that 'Christianity and Culture' came fairly early in Lewis's theological corpus. It might best be considered an early step in his spiritual pilgrimage—but certainly not his arrival. Here, instead of spirit progressively irradiating and transforming soul, he seems to envisage a relation between them in strict terms of 'either-or', with soul as Calvin's 'nature' and spirit as his 'grace', and spirit beginning exactly where soul leaves off. Later on he dealt much more profoundly with the relation between soul and spirit in such things as the essay on 'Transposition' and *The Four Loves*. He says, for instance, in 'Transposition':

> May we not ... suppose ... that there is no experience of the spirit so transcendent and supernatural, no vision of Deity Himself so close and so far beyond all images and emotions, that to it also there cannot be an appropriate correspondence on the sensory level? Not by a new sense but by the incredible flooding of those very sensations we now have with a meaning, a transvaluation, of which we have here no faintest guess?[1]

[1] 'Transposition', *Transposition and Other Addresses*, London: Geoffrey Bles Ltd. (1949), p. 20. An expanded version of this essay appears in *Screwtape Proposes a Toast and Other Pieces*, London: Fontana Books (1965).

xii

(3) 'Religion: Reality or Substitute?' is reprinted from the now extinct *World Dominion*, vol. XIX (Sept.-Oct. 1941), except for the autobiographical paragraph 4 and part of paragraph 9 which were added a few years later. (4) The essay on 'Ethics' is published here for the first time. As I have suggested in a footnote (p. 47), I believe this paper to have been written before Lewis's *Abolition of Man* (1943); if I am right, it appears in the correct chronological sequence. (5) *'De Futilitate'* is an address given at Magdalen College, Oxford, during the Second World War at the invitation of Sir Henry Tizard (then President of Magdalen College). It, too, is published for the first time. (6) 'The Poison of Subjectivism' is reprinted from *Religion in Life*, vol. XII (Summer 1943).

(7) 'The Funeral of a Great Myth', published for the first time, may appear an intruder on theological premises. I have included it here because the 'myth' discussed in this essay seems quite obviously to be an outgrowth and development of one of the myths compared to the Christian Faith in Lewis's 'Is Theology Poetry?' (*The Socratic Digest*, No. 3 (1945), pp. 25-35.). Its close connection with the *Digest* essay caused me to feel it deserved a place here; it is, also, relevant to the idea of Theism. (8) 'On Church Music' is reprinted from *English Church Music*, vol. XIX (April 1949). Lewis did not himself like hymns and the existence of this paper is entirely owing to the special invitation of his friend, Mr Leonard Blake, who was editor of *English Church Music* at the time. (9) 'Historicism' originally appeared in *The Month*, vol. IV (October 1950).

(10) The two-part essay on 'The Psalms' is published for the first time. Judging from the handwriting (Lewis wrote all his works by hand), it roughly corresponds in time with the publication of his book, *Reflections on the Psalms* (1958). By the by, Lewis and T. S. Eliot met one another for the first time in 1961 at Lambeth Palace where they worked together on the Archbishops of Canterbury and York's Commission for the Revision of the Psalter. (11) Although two pages of the manuscript of 'The Language of Religion' are lost, the omission, fortunately, does not seriously affect the main argument of the paper. It appears in print for the first time, as does (12) 'Petitionary Prayer: A Problem without an Answer' which was originally read to the Oxford Clerical Society on 8th December 1953. (13) 'Modern Theology

and Biblical Criticism' is the title I have given to a paper Lewis read at Westcott House, Cambridge, on 11th May 1959. This is its first publication. (14) 'The Seeing Eye' was originally published in the American periodical, *Show*, vol. III (Feb. 1963) under the title 'Onward, Christian Spacemen'. Lewis so heartily disliked the title which the editors of *Show* gave this piece that I felt justified in re-naming it.

As Lewis did not prepare these essays for publication, I have ventured to add here and there a footnote where references might be useful and to draw attention to other works by Lewis on the same subject. My own notes are enclosed within square brackets in order to prevent their being confused with Lewis's.

My thanks go to Major W. H. Lewis to whom I owe the honour of serving as his late brother's editor. I have received so much help and kindness from Mr Owen Barfield and Dr and Mrs Austin Farrer that I gratefully record my obligation to them. I also express my gratitude to Miss Jackie Gibbs who assisted me with the typing. Finally, it is a pleasure to thank Mr Daryl R. Williams of my College who has so conscientiously corrected the proofs to this book.

Wadham College, Oxford.   WALTER HOOPER
St Michael and All Angels, 1966

CHRISTIANITY AND LITERATURE

When I was asked to address this society, I was at first tempted to refuse because the subject proposed to me, that of Christianity and Literature, did not seem to admit of any discussion. I knew, of course, that Christian story and sentiment were among the things on which literature could be written, and, conversely, that literature was one of the ways in which Christian sentiment could be expressed and Christian story told; but there seemed nothing more to be said of Christianity in this connection than of any of the hundred and one other things that men made books about. We are familiar, no doubt, with the expression 'Christian Art', by which people usually mean Art that represents Biblical or hagiological scenes, and there is, in this sense, a fair amount of 'Christian Literature'. But I question whether it has any literary qualities peculiar to itself. The rules for writing a good passion play or a good devotional lyric are simply the rules for writing tragedy or lyric in general: success in sacred literature depends on the same qualities of structure, suspense, variety, diction, and the like which secure success in secular literature. And if we enlarge the idea of Christian Literature to include not only literature on sacred themes but all that is written by Christians for Christians to read, then, I think, Christian Literature can exist only in the same sense in which Christian cookery might exist. It would be possible, and it might be edifying, to write a Christian cookery book. Such a book would exclude dishes whose preparation involves unnecessary human labour or animal suffering, and dishes excessively luxurious. That is to say, its choice of dishes would be Christian. But there could be nothing specifically Christian about the actual cooking of the dishes included. Boiling an egg is the same process whether you are a Christian or a Pagan. In the same way, literature written by Christians for Christians would have to avoid mendacity, cruelty, blasphemy, pornography, and the like, and it would aim at edification in so far as edification was proper to the kind of work in hand. But whatever it chose to do would have to

I

be done by the means common to all literature; it could succeed or fail only by the same excellences and the same faults as all literature; and its literary success or failure would never be the same thing as its obedience or disobedience to Christian principles.

I have been speaking so far of Christian Literature *proprement dite*—that is, of writing which is intended to affect us as literature, by its appeal to imagination. But in the visible arts I think we can make a distinction between sacred art, however sacred in theme, and pure iconography—between that which is intended, in the first instance, to affect the imagination and the aesthetic appetite, and that which is meant merely as the starting-point for devotion and meditation. If I were treating the visible arts I should have to work out here a full distinction of the work of art from the icon on the one hand and the toy on the other. The icon and the toy have this in common that their value depends very little on their perfection as artefacts—a shapeless rag may give as much pleasure as the costliest doll, and two sticks tied crosswise may kindle as much devotion as the work of Leonardo.[1] And to make matters more complicated the very same object could often be used in all three ways. But I do not think the icon and the work of art can be so sharply distinguished in literature. I question whether the badness of a really bad hymn can ordinarily be so irrelevant to devotion as the badness of a bad devotional picture. Because the hymn uses words, its badness will, to some degree, consist in confused or erroneous thought and unworthy sentiment. But I mention this difficult question here only to say that I do not propose to treat it. If any literary works exist which have a purely iconographic value and no literary value, they are not what I am

[1 Cf. Lewis's 'How the Few and the Many Use Pictures and Music' in *An Experiment in Criticism* (Cambridge, 1961), pp. 17–18: 'The Teddy-bear exists in order that the child may endow it with imaginary life and personality and enter into a quasi-social relationship with it. That is what "playing with it" means. The better this activity succeeds the less the actual appearance of the object will matter. Too close or prolonged attention to its changeless and expressionless face impedes the play. A crucifix exists in order to direct the worshipper's thought and affections to the Passion. It had better not have any excellencies, subtleties, or originalities which will fix attention upon itself. Hence devout people may, for this purpose, prefer the crudest and emptiest icon. The emptier, the more permeable; and they want, as it were, to pass through the material image and go beyond.']

talking about. Indeed I could not, for I have not met them.

Of Christian Literature, then, in the sense of 'work aiming at literary value and written by Christians for Christians', you see that I have really nothing to say and believe that nothing can be said. But I think I have something to say about what may be called the Christian approach to literature: about the principles, if you will, of Christian literary theory and criticism. For while I was thinking over the subject you gave me I made what seemed to me a discovery. It is not an easy one to put into words. The nearest I can come to it is to say that I found a disquieting contrast between the whole circle of ideas used in modern criticism and certain ideas recurrent in the New Testament. Let me say at once that it is hardly a question of logical contradiction between clearly defined concepts. It is too vague for that. It is more a repugnance of atmospheres, a discordance of notes, an incompatibility of temperaments.

What are the key-words of modern criticism? *Creative*, with its opposite *derivative*; *spontaneity*, with its opposite *convention*; *freedom*, contrasted with *rules*. Great authors are innovators, pioneers, explorers; bad authors bunch in schools and follow models. Or again, great authors are always 'breaking fetters' and 'bursting bonds'. They have personality, they 'are themselves'. I do not know whether we often think out the implication of such language into a consistent philosophy; but we certainly have a general picture of bad work flowing from conformity and discipleship, and of good work bursting out from certain centres of explosive force—apparently self-originating force—which we call men of genius.

Now the New Testament has nothing at all to tell us of literature. I know that there are some who like to think of Our Lord Himself as a poet and cite the parables to support their view. I admit freely that to believe in the Incarnation at all is to believe that every mode of human excellence is implicit in His historical human character: poethood, of course, included. But if all had been developed, the limitations of a single human life would have been transcended and He would not have been a man; therefore all excellences save the spiritual remained in varying degrees implicit. If it is claimed that the poetic excellence is more developed than others—say, the intellectual—I think I deny the claim.

3

Some of the parables do work like poetic similes; but then others work like philosophic illustrations. Thus the Unjust Judge is not emotionally or imaginatively like God: he corresponds to God as the terms in a proportion correspond, because he is to the Widow (in one highly specialized respect) as God is to man. In that parable Our Lord, if we may so express it, is much more like Socrates than Shakespeare. And I dread an over-emphasis on the poetical element in His words because I think it tends to obscure that quality in His human character which is, in fact, so visible in His irony, His *argumenta ad homines*, and His use of the *a fortiori*, and which I would call the homely, peasant shrewdness. Donne points out that we are never told He laughed; it is difficult in reading the Gospels not to believe, and to tremble in believing, that He smiled.

I repeat, the New Testament has nothing to say of literature; but what it says on other subjects is quite sufficient to strike that note which I find out of tune with the language of modern criticism. I must begin with something that is unpopular. St Paul tells us (I Cor, xi, 3) that man is the 'head' of woman. We may soften this if we like by saying that he means only man *quâ* man and woman *quâ* woman and that an equality of the sexes as citizens or intellectual beings is not therefore absolutely repugnant to his thought: indeed, that he himself tells us that in another respect, that is 'in the Lord', the sexes cannot be thus separated (*ibid.*, xi, 11). But what concerns me here is to find out what he means by Head. Now in verse 3 he has given us a very remarkable proportion sum: that God is to Christ as Christ is to man and man is to woman, and the relation between each term and the next is that of Head. And in verse 7 we are told that man is God's image and glory, and woman is man's glory. He does not repeat 'image', but I question whether the omission is intentional, and I suggest that we shall have a fairly Pauline picture of this whole series of Head relations running from God to woman if we picture each term as the 'image and glory' of the preceding term. And I suppose that of which one is the image and glory is that which one glorifies by copying or imitating. Let me once again insist that I am not trying to twist St Paul's metaphors into a logical system. I know well that whatever picture he is building up, he himself will be the first to throw it aside when it has served its turn and to

4

adopt some quite different picture when some new aspect of the truth is present to his mind. But I want to see clearly the sort of picture implied in this passage—to get it clear however temporary its use or partial its application. And it seems to me a quite clear picture; we are to think of some original divine virtue passing downwards from rung to rung of a hierarchical ladder, and the mode in which each lower rung receives it is, quite frankly, imitation.

What is perhaps most startling in this picture is the apparent equivalence of the woman–man and man–God relation with the relation between Christ and God, or, in Trinitarian language, with the relation between the First and Second Persons of the Trinity. As a layman and a comparatively recently reclaimed apostate I have, of course, no intention of building a theological system— still less of setting up a *catena* of New Testament metaphors as a criticism on the Nicene or the Athanasian creed, documents which I wholly accept. But it is legitimate to notice what kinds of metaphor the New Testament uses; more especially when what we are in search of is not dogma but a kind of flavour or atmosphere. And there is no doubt that this kind of proportion sum— A:B: :B:C—is quite freely used in the New Testament where A and B represent the First and Second Persons of the Trinity. Thus St Paul has already told us earlier in the same epistle that we are 'of Christ' and Christ is 'of God' (iii, 23). Thus again in the Fourth Gospel, Our Lord Himself compares the relation of the Father to the Son with that of the Son to His flock, in respect of knowledge (x, 15) and of love (xv, 9).

I suggest, therefore, that this picture of a hierarchical order in which we are encouraged—though, of course, only from certain points of view and in certain respects—to regard the Second Person Himself as a step, or stage, or degree, is wholly in accord with the spirit of the New Testament. And if we ask how the stages are connected the answer always seems to be something like imitation, reflection, assimilation. Thus in Gal. iv, 19, Christ is to be 'formed' inside each believer—the verb here used ($\mu o \rho \phi \omega \theta \hat{\eta}$) meaning to shape, to figure, or even to draw a sketch. In First Thessalonians (i, 6) Christians are told to imitate St Paul and the Lord, and elsewhere (1 Cor. xi, 1) to imitate St Paul as he in turn imitates Christ—thus giving us another stage of progressive imitation. Changing the metaphor we find that believers are to acquire the fragrance of Christ, *redolere Christum* (2 Cor. ii, 16): that the glory of God has appeared in the face of Christ as, at the creation, light appeared in the universe (2 Cor. iv, 6); and, finally, if my reading of a much disputed passage is correct, that a Christian is to Christ as a mirror to an object (2 Cor. iii, 18).

These passages, you will notice, are all Pauline; but there is a place in the Fourth Gospel which goes much farther—so far that if it were not a Dominical utterance we would not venture to think along such lines. There (v. 19) we are told that the Son does only what He sees the Father doing. He watches the Father's operations and does the same (ὁμοίως ποιεῖ) or 'copies'. The Father, because of His love for the Son, shows Him all that He does. I have already explained that I am not a theologian. What aspect of the Trinitarian reality Our Lord, as God, saw while He spoke these words, I do not venture to define; but I think we have a right and even a duty to notice carefully the earthly image by which He expressed it—to see clearly the picture He puts before us. It is a picture of a boy learning to do things by watching a man at work. I think we may even guess what memory, humanly speaking, was in His mind. It is hard not to imagine that He remembered His boyhood, that He saw Himself as a boy in a carpenter's shop, a boy learning how to do things by watching while St Joseph did them. So taken, the passage does not seem to me to conflict with anything I have learned from the creeds, but greatly to enrich my conception of the Divine sonship.

Now it may be that there is no absolute logical contradiction between the passages I have quoted and the assumptions of modern criticism: but I think there is so great a difference of temper that a man whose mind was at one with the mind of the New Testament would not, and indeed could not, fall into the language which most critics now adopt. In the New Testament the art of life itself is an art of imitation: can we, believing this, believe that literature, which must derive from real life, is to aim at being 'creative', 'original', and 'spontaneous'. 'Originality' in the New Testament is quite plainly the prerogative of God alone; even within the triune being of God it seems to be confined to the Father. The duty and happiness of every other being is placed in being derivative, in reflecting like a mirror. Nothing could be more foreign to the tone of scripture than the language of those who describe a saint as a 'moral genius' or a 'spiritual genius' thus insinuating that his virtue or spirituality is 'creative' or 'original'. If I have read the New Testament aright, it leaves no room for 'creativeness' even in a modified or metaphorical sense. Our whole destiny seems to lie in the opposite direction, in being as little as possible ourselves, in acquiring a fragrance that is not our own but borrowed, in becoming clean mirrors filled with the image of a face that is not ours. I am not here supporting the doctrine of total depravity, and I do not say that the New Testament supports it; I am saying only that the highest good of a creature must be creaturely—that is, derivative or reflective—good. In other words, as St Augustine makes plain (*De Civ. Dei* xii, cap. I), pride does not only go before a fall but is a fall—a fall of the creature's attention from what is better, God, to what is worse, itself.

Applying this principle to literature, in its greatest generality, we should get as the basis of all critical theory the maxim that an author should never conceive himself as bringing into existence beauty or wisdom which did not exist before, but simply and solely as trying to embody in terms of his own art some reflection of eternal Beauty and Wisdom. Our criticism would therefore from the beginning group itself with some existing theories of poetry against others. It would have affinities with the primitive or Homeric theory in which the poet is the mere pensioner of the Muse. It would have affinities with the Platonic doctrine of a transcendent Form partly imitable on earth; and remoter affinities with the Aristotelian doctrine of μίμησις and the Augustan doctrine about the imitation of Nature and the Ancients. It would be opposed to the theory of genius as, perhaps, generally understood; and above all it would be opposed to the idea that literature is self-expression.

But here some distinctions must be made. I spoke just now of the ancient idea that the poet was merely the servant of some god, of Apollo, or the Muse; but let us not forget the highly paradoxical words in which Homer's Phemius asserts his claim to be a poet—

Αὐτοδίδακτος δ' εἰμί, θεὸς δέ μοι ἐν φρεσὶν οἴμας
Παντοίας ἐνέφυσεν. (*Od.* xxii, 347.)

7

'I am self-taught; a god has inspired me with all manner of songs.'
It sounds like a direct contradiction. How can he be self-taught
if the god has taught him all he knows? Doubtless because the
god's instruction is given internally, not through the senses, and is
therefore regarded as part of the Self, to be contrasted with such
external aids as, say, the example of other poets. And this seems
to blur the distinction I am trying to draw between Christian
imitation and the 'originality' praised by modern critics. Phemius
obviously claims to be original, in the sense of being no other
poet's disciple, and in the same breath admits his complete de-
pendence on a supernatural teacher. Does not this let in 'originality' and 'creativeness' of the only kind that have ever been
claimed?

If you said: 'The only kind that ought to have been claimed', I
would agree; but as things are, I think the distinction remains,
though it becomes finer than our first glance suggested. A
Christian and an unbelieving poet may both be equally original
in the sense that they neglect the example of their poetic forbears
and draw on resources peculiar to themselves, but with this
difference. The unbeliever may take his own temperament and
experience, just as they happen to stand, and consider them worth
communicating simply because they are facts or, worse still,
because they are his. To the Christian his own temperament and
experience, as mere fact, and as merely his, are of no value or
importance whatsoever: he will deal with them, if at all, only
because they are the medium through which, or the position
from which, something universally profitable appeared to him.
We can imagine two men seated in different parts of a church or
theatre. Both, when they come out, may tell us their experiences,
and both may use the first person. But the one is interested in his
seat only because it was his—'I was most uncomfortable', he will
say. 'You would hardly believe what a draught comes in from
the door in that corner. And the people! I had to speak pretty
sharply to the woman in front of me.' The other will tell us what
could be seen from his seat, choosing to describe this because this
is what he knows, and because every seat must give the best view
of something. 'Do you know', he will begin, 'the moulding on
those pillars goes on round at the back. It looks, too, as if the
design on the back were the older of the two.' Here we have the

8

expressionist and the Christian attitudes towards the self or temperament. Thus St Augustine and Rousseau both write *Confessions*; but to the one his own temperament is a kind of absolute (*au moins je suis autre*), to the other it is 'a narrow house too narrow for Thee to enter—oh make it wide. It is in ruins—oh rebuild it.' And Wordsworth, the romantic who made a good end, has a foot in either world and though he practises both, distinguishes well the two ways in which a man may be said to write about himself. On the one hand he says:

> [For] I must tread on shadowy ground, must sink
> Deep, and aloft ascending breathe in worlds
> To which the heaven of heavens is but a veil.[1]

On the other he craves indulgence if

> with this
> I mix[2] more lowly matter; with the thing
> Contemplated, describe the Mind and Man
> Contemplating; and who and what he was—
> The transitory being that beheld
> This vision.[3]

In this sense, then, the Christian writer may be self-taught or original. He may base his work on the 'transitory being' that he is, not because he thinks it valuable (for he knows that in his flesh dwells no good thing), but solely because of the 'vision' that appeared to it. But he will have no preference for doing this. He will do it if it happens to be the thing he can do best; but if his talents are such that he can produce good work by writing in an established form and dealing with experiences common to all his race, he will do so just as gladly. I even think he will do so more gladly. It is to him an argument not of strength but of weakness that he should respond fully to the vision only 'in his own way'. And always, of every idea and of every method he will ask not 'Is it mine?', but 'Is it good?'

[1] *The Recluse*, Part I, Book I 11. 772–74, from Appendix A in *The Poetical Works of William Wordsworth*, vol. V, ed. E. de Selincourt and Helen Darbishire (Oxford, 1949).]

[2] 'Mix' is, I think, a scribal error for Wordsworth's 'blend' as given in the de Selincourt and Darbishire edition.]

[3] *op. cit.*, 11. 829–34.]

This seems to me the most fundamental difference between the Christian and the unbeliever in their approach to literature. But I think there is another. The Christian will take literature a little less seriously than the cultured Pagan: he will feel less uneasy with a purely hedonistic standard for at least many kinds of work. The unbeliever is always apt to make a kind of religion of his aesthetic experiences; he feels ethically irresponsible, perhaps, but he braces his strength to receive responsibilities of another kind which seem to the Christian quite illusory. He has to be 'creative'; he has to obey a mystical amoral law called his artistic conscience; and he commonly wishes to maintain his superiority to the great mass of mankind who turn to books for mere recreation. But the Christian knows from the outset that the salvation of a single soul is more important than the production or preservation of all the epics and tragedies in the world: and as for superiority, he knows that the vulgar since they include most of the poor probably include most of his superiors. He has no objection to comedies that merely amuse and tales that merely refresh; for he thinks like Thomas Aquinas *ipsa ratio hoc habet ut quandoque rationis usus intercipiatur.* We can play, as we can eat, to the glory of God. It thus may come about that Christian views on literature will strike the world as shallow and flippant; but the world must not misunderstand. When Christian work is done on a serious subject there is no gravity and no sublimity it cannot attain. But they will belong to the theme. That is why they will be real and lasting— mighty nouns with which literature, an adjectival thing, is here united, far over-topping the fussy and ridiculous claims of literature that tries to be important simply as literature. And *a posteriori* it is not hard to argue that all the greatest poems have been made by men who valued something else much more than poetry—even if that something else were only cutting down enemies in a cattle-raid or tumbling a girl in a bed. The real frivolity, the solemn vacuity, is all with those who make literature a self-existent thing to be valued for its own sake. Pater prepared for pleasure as if it were martyrdom.

Now that I see where I have arrived a doubt assails me. It all sounds suspiciously like things I have said before, starting from very different premisses. Is it King Charles's Head? Have I mistaken for the 'vision' the same old 'transitory being' who, in some ways, is not nearly transitory enough? It may be so: or I may, after all be right. I would rather be right if I could; but if not, if I have only been once more following my own footprints, it is the sort of tragi-comedy which, on my own principles, I must try to enjoy. I find a beautiful example proposed in the *Paradiso* (XXVIII) where poor Pope Gregory, arrived in Heaven, discovered that his theory of the hierarchies, on which presumably he had taken pains, was quite wrong. We are told how the redeemed soul behaved; '*di sè medesmo rise*'. It was the funniest thing he'd ever heard.

CHRISTIANITY AND CULTURE

'If the heavenly life is not grown up in you, it signifies nothing what you have chosen in the stead of it, or why you have chosen it.'

—WILLIAM LAW

At an early age I came to believe that the life of culture (that is, of intellectual and aesthetic activity) was very good for its own sake, or even that it was the good for man. After my conversion, which occurred in my later twenties, I continued to hold this belief without consciously asking how it could be reconciled with my new belief that the end of human life was salvation in Christ and the glorifying of God. I was awakened from this confused state of mind by finding that the friends of culture seemed to me to be exaggerating. In my reaction against what seemed exaggerated I was driven to the other extreme, and began, in my own mind, to belittle the claims of culture. As soon as I did this I was faced with the question, 'If it is a thing of so little value, how are you justified in spending so much of your life on it?'

The present inordinate esteem of culture by the cultured began, I think, with Matthew Arnold—at least if I am right in supposing that he first popularized the use of the English word *spiritual* in the sense of German *geistlich*. This was nothing less than the identification of levels of life hitherto usually distinguished. After Arnold came the vogue of Croce, in whose philosophy the aesthetic and logical activities were made autonomous forms of 'the spirit' co-ordinate with the ethical. There followed the poetics of Dr I. A. Richards. This great atheist critic found in a good poetical taste the means of attaining psychological adjustments which improved a man's power of effective and satisfactory living all round, while bad taste resulted in a corresponding loss. Since this theory of value was a purely psychological one, this amounted to giving poetry a kind of soteriological function; it held the keys of the only heaven that Dr Richards believed in. His work (which

I respect profoundly) was continued, though not always in directions that he accepted, by the editors of Scrutiny,[1] who believe in 'a necessary relationship between the quality of the individual's response to art and his general fitness for humane living'. Finally, as might have been expected, a somewhat similar view was expressed by a Christian writer: in fact by Brother Every in Theology for March, 1939. In an article entitled 'The Necessity of Scrutiny' Brother Every inquired what Mr Eliot's admirers were to think of a Church where those who seemed to be theologically equipped preferred Housman, Mr Charles Morgan, and Miss Sayers, to Lawrence, Joyce and Mr E. M. Forster; he spoke (I think with sympathy) of the 'sensitive questioning individual' who is puzzled at finding the same judgements made by Christians as by 'other conventional people'; and he talked of 'testing' theological students as regards their power to evaluate a new piece of writing on a secular subject.

As soon as I read this there was the devil to pay. I was not sure that I understood—I am still not sure that I understand—Brother Every's position. But I felt that some readers might easily get the notion that 'sensitivity' or good taste were among the notes of the true Church, or that coarse, unimaginative people were less likely to be saved than refined and poetic people. In the heat of the moment I rushed to the opposite extreme. I felt, with some spiritual pride, that I had been saved in the nick of time from being 'sensitive'. The 'sentimentality and cheapness' of much Christian hymnody had been a strong point in my own resistance to conversion. Now I felt almost thankful for the bad hymns.[2] It was good that we should have to lay down our precious refinement at the very doorstep of the church; good that we should be cured at the outset of our inveterate confusion between psyche and pneuma, nature and supernature.

[1] I take Scrutiny throughout as it is represented in Brother Every's article. An independent criticism of that periodical is no part of my purpose.

[2] We should be cautious of assuming that we know what their most banal expressions actually stand for in the minds of uneducated, holy persons. Of a saint's conversation Patmore says: 'He will most likely dwell with reiteration on commonplaces with which you were perfectly acquainted before you were twelve years old; but you must ... remember that the knowledge which is to you a superficies is to him a solid' (Rod, Root and Flower, Magna Moralia, xiv).

A man is never so proud as when striking an attitude of humility. Brother Every will not suspect me of being still in the condition I describe, nor of still attributing to him the preposterous beliefs I have just suggested. But there remains, none the less, a real problem which his article forced upon me in its most acute form. No one, presumably, is really maintaining that a fine taste in the arts is a condition of salvation. Yet the glory of God, and, as our only means to glorifying Him, the salvation of human souls, is the real business of life. What, then, is the value of culture? It is, of course, no new question; but as a living question it was new to me.

I naturally turned first to the New Testament. Here I found, in the first place, a demand that whatever is most highly valued on the natural level is to be held, as it were, merely on sufferance, and to be abandoned without mercy the moment it conflicts with the service of God. The organs of sense (Matt. v, 29) and of virility (Matt. xix, 12) may have to be sacrificed. And I took it that the least these words could mean was that a life, by natural standards, crippled and thwarted was not only no bar to salvation, but might easily be one of its conditions. The text about hating father and mother (Luke xiv, 26) and our Lord's apparent belittling even of His own natural relation to the Blessed Virgin (Matt. xii, 48) were even more discouraging. I took it for granted that anyone in his senses would hold it better to be a good son than a good critic, and that whatever was said of natural affection was implied a fortiori of culture. The worst of all was Philippians iii, 8, where something obviously more relevant to spiritual life than culture can be—'blameless' conformity to the Jewish Law—was described as 'muck'.

In the second place I found a number of emphatic warnings against every kind of superiority. We were told to become as children (Matt. xviii, 3), not to be called Rabbi (Matt. xxiii, 8), to dread reputation (Luke vi, 26). We were reminded that few of the σοφοὶ κατὰ σάρκα—which, I suppose, means precisely the intelligentsia—are called (1 Cor. i, 26); that a man must become a fool by secular standards before he can attain real wisdom (1 Cor. iii, 18).

Against all this I found some passages that could be interpreted in a sense more favourable to culture. I argued that secular learning might be embodied in the Magi; that the Talents in the parable might conceivably include 'talents' in the modern sense of the word; that the miracle at Cana in Galilee by sanctifying an innocent, sensuous pleasure[1] could be taken to sanctify at least a recreational use of culture—mere 'entertainment'; and that aesthetic enjoyment of nature was certainly hallowed by our Lord's praise of the lilies. At least some use of science was implied in St Paul's demand that we should perceive the Invisible through the visible (Rom. i, 20). But I was more than doubtful whether his exhortation, 'Be not children in mind' (1 Cor. xiv, 20), and his boast of 'wisdom' among the initiate, referred to anything that we should recognize as secular culture.

On the whole, the New Testament seemed, if not hostile, yet unmistakably cold to culture. I think we can still believe culture to be innocent after we have read the New Testament; I cannot see that we are encouraged to think it important.

It might be important none the less, for Hooker has finally answered the contention that Scripture must contain everything important or even everything necessary. Remembering this, I continued my researches. If my selection of authorities seems arbitrary, that is due not to a bias but to my ignorance. I used such authors as I happened to know.

Of the great pagans Aristotle is on our side. Plato will tolerate no culture that does not directly or indirectly conduce either to the intellectual vision of the good or the military efficiency of the commonwealth. Joyce and D. H. Lawrence would have fared ill in the Republic. The Buddha was, I believe, anti-cultural, but here especially I speak under correction.

St Augustine regarded the liberal education which he had undergone in his boyhood as a *dementia*, and wondered why it should be considered *honestior et uberior* than the really useful 'primary' education which preceded it (*Conf.* I, xiii). He is extremely distrustful of his own delight in church music (*ibid.*, X, xxxiii). Tragedy (which for Dr Richards is 'a great exercise of the spirit')[2] is for St Augustine a kind of sore. The spectator suffers, yet loves his suffering, and this is a *miserabilis insania* . . .

---

[1] On a possible deeper significance in this miracle, see F. Mauriac, *Vie de Jésus*, cap. 5, *ad fin.*

[2] *Principles of Literary Criticism*, p. 69.

quid autem mirum cum infelix pecus aberrans a grege tuo et inpatiens custodiae tuae turpi scabie foedarer (ibid., III, ii).

St Jerome, allegorizing the parable of the Prodigal Son, suggests that the husks with which he was fain to fill his belly may signify *cibus daemonum . . . carmina poetarum, saecularis sapientia, rhetoricorum pompa verborum* (Ep. xxi, 4).

Let none reply that the Fathers were speaking of polytheistic literature at a time when polytheism was still a danger. The scheme of values presupposed in most imaginative literature has not become very much more Christian since the time of St Jerome. In *Hamlet* we see everything questioned *except* the duty of revenge. In all Shakespeare's works the conception of good really operative—whatever the characters may say—seems to be purely worldly. In medieval romance, honour and sexual love are the true values; in nineteenth-century fiction, sexual love and material prosperity. In romantic poetry, either the enjoyment of nature (ranging from pantheistic mysticism at one end of the scale to mere innocent sensuousness at the other) or else the indulgence of a *Sehnsucht* awakened by the past, the distant, and the imagined, but not believed, supernatural. In modern literature, the life of liberated instinct. There are, of course, exceptions: but to study these exceptions would not be to study literature as such, and as a whole. 'All literatures', as Newman has said,[1] 'are one; they are the voices of the natural man . . . if Literature is to be made a study of human nature, you cannot have a Christian Literature. It is a contradiction in terms to attempt a sinless Literature of sinful man.' And I could not doubt that the sub-Christian or anti-Christian values implicit in most literature did actually infect many readers. Only a few days ago I was watching, in some scholarship papers, the results of this infection in a belief that the crimes of such Shakespearian characters as Cleopatra and Macbeth were somehow compensated for by a quality described as their 'greatness'. This very morning I have read in a critic the remark that if the wicked lovers in Webster's *White Devil* had repented we should hardly have forgiven them. And many people certainly draw from Keats's phrase about negative capability or 'love of good and evil' (if the reading which attributes to him such meaningless words is correct) a strange doctrine that ex-

[1] *Scope and Nature of University Education.* Discourse 8.

perience *simpliciter* is good. I do not say that the sympathetic reading of literature must produce such results, but that it may and often does. If we are to answer the Fathers' attack on pagan literature we must not ground our answer on a belief that literature as a whole has become, in any important sense, more Christian since their days.

In Thomas Aquinas I could not find anything directly bearing on my problem; but I am a very poor Thomist and shall be grateful for correction on this point.

Thomas à Kempis I take to be definitely on the anti-cultural side.

In the *Theologia Germanica* (cap. xx) I found that nature's refusal of the life of Christ 'happeneth most of all where there are high natural gifts of reason, for that soareth upwards in its own light and by its own power, till at last it cometh to think itself the true Eternal Light'. But in a later chapter (xlii) I found the evil of the false light identified with its tendency to love knowledge and discernment more than the object known and discerned. This seemed to point to the possibility of a knowledge which avoided that error.

The cumulative effect of all this was very discouraging to culture. On the other side—perhaps only through the accidental distribution of my ignorance—I found much less.

I found the famous saying, attributed to Gregory, that our use of secular culture was comparable to the action of the Israelites in going down to the Philistines to have their knives sharpened. This seems to me a most satisfactory argument as far as it goes, and very relevant to modern conditions. If we are to convert our heathen neighbours, we must understand their culture. We must 'beat them at their own game'. But of course, while this would justify Christian culture (at least for some Christians whose vocation lay in that direction) at the moment, it would come very far short of the claims made for culture in our modern tradition. On the Gregorian view culture is a weapon; and a weapon is essentially a thing we lay aside as soon as we safely can.

In Milton I found a disquieting ally. His *Areopagitica* troubled me just as Brother Every's article had troubled me. He seemed to make too little of the difficulties; and his glorious defence of freedom to explore all good and evil seemed, after all, to be based on an aristocratic preoccupation with great souls and a contemptuous indifference to the mass of mankind which, I suppose, no Christian can tolerate.

Finally I came to that book of Newman's from which I have already quoted, the lectures on *University Education*. Here at last I found an author who seemed to be aware of both sides of the question; for no one ever insisted so eloquently as Newman on the beauty of culture for its own sake, and no one ever so sternly resisted the temptation to confuse it with things spiritual. The cultivation of the intellect, according to him, is 'for this world':[1] between it and 'genuine religion' there is a 'radical difference';[2] it makes 'not the Christian . . . but the gentleman', and looks like virtue 'only at a distance';[3] he 'will not for an instant allow' that it makes men better.[4] The 'pastors of the Church' may indeed welcome culture because it provides innocent distraction at those moments of spiritual relaxation which would otherwise very likely lead to sin; and in this way it often 'draws the mind off from things which will harm it to subjects worthy of a rational being'. But even in so doing 'it does not raise it above nature, nor has any tendency to make us pleasing to our Maker'.[5] In some instances the cultural and the spiritual value of an activity may even be in inverse ratio. Theology, when it ceases to be part of liberal knowledge, and is pursued for purely pastoral ends, gains in 'meritoriousness' but loses in liberality 'just as a face worn by tears and fasting loses its beauty'.[6] On the other hand Newman is certain that liberal knowlege is an end in itself; the whole of the fourth Discourse is devoted to this theme. The solution of this apparent antinomy lies in his doctrine that everything, including, of course, the intellect, 'has its own perfection. Things animate, inanimate, visible, invisible, all are good in their kind, and have a *best* of themselves, which is an object of pursuit.'[7] To perfect the mind is 'an object as intelligible as the cultivation of virtue, while, at the same time, it is absolutely distinct from it'.[8]

Whether because I am too poor a theologian to understand the implied doctrine of grace and nature, or for some other reason, I have not been able to make Newman's conclusion my

[1] *Op. cit.*, VIII, p. 227, in Everyman Edition.
[2] VII, p. 184, 5.   [3] IV, p. 112.   [4] IV, p. 111.   [5] VII, p. 180.
[6] IV, p. 100.   [7] IV, p. 113.   [8] IV, p. 114.

own. I can well understand that there is a kind of goodness which is not moral; as a well-grown healthy toad is 'better' or 'more perfect' than a three-legged toad, or an archangel is 'better' than an angel. In this sense a clever man is 'better' than a dull one, or any man than any chimpanzee. The trouble comes when we start asking how much of our time and energy God wants us to spend in becoming 'better' or 'more perfect' in this sense. If Newman is right in saying that culture has *no* tendency 'to make us pleasing to our Maker', then the answer would seem to be, 'None.' And that is a tenable view: as though God said, 'Your *natural* degree of perfection, your place in the chain of being, is my affair: do you get on with what I have explicitly left as your task—righteousness.' But if Newman had thought this he would not, I suppose, have written the discourse on 'Liberal Knowledge its Own End'. On the other hand, it would be possible to hold (perhaps it is pretty generally held) that one of the moral duties of a rational creature was to attain to the highest non-moral perfection it could. But if this were so, then (*a*) The perfecting of the mind would not be 'absolutely distinct' from virtue but part of the content of virtue; and (*b*) It would be very odd that Scripture and the tradition of the Church have little or nothing to say about this duty. I am afraid that Newman has left the problem very much where he found it. He has clarified our minds by explaining that culture gives us a non-moral 'perfection'. But on the real problem—that of relating such non-moral values to the duty or interest of creatures who are every minute advancing either to heaven or hell—he seems to help little. 'Sensitivity' may be a perfection: but if by becoming sensitive I neither please God nor save my soul, why should I become sensitive? Indeed, what exactly is meant by a 'perfection' compatible with utter loss of the end for which I was created?

My researches left me with the impression that there could be no question of restoring to culture the kind of status which I had given it before my conversion. If any constructive case for culture was to be built up it would have to be of a much humbler kind; and the whole tradition of educated infidelity from Arnold to *Scrutiny* appeared to me as but one phase in that general rebellion against God which began in the eighteenth century. In this mood I set about construction.

1. I begin at the lowest and least ambitious level. My own professional work, though conditioned by taste and talents, is immediately motivated by the need for earning my living. And on earning one's living I was relieved to note that Christianity, in spite of its revolutionary and apocalyptic elements, can be delightfully humdrum. The Baptist did not give the tax-gatherers and soldiers lectures on the immediate necessity of turning the economic and military system of the ancient world upside down; he told them to obey the moral law—as they had presumably learned it from their mothers and nurses—and sent them back to their jobs. St Paul advised the Thessalonians to stick to their work (1 Thess. iv, 11) and not to become busybodies (2 Thess. iii, 11). The need for money is therefore *simpliciter* an innocent, though by no means a splendid, motive for any occupation. The Ephesians are warned to work professionally at something that is 'good' (Eph. iv, 28). I hoped that 'good' here did not mean much more than 'harmless', and I was certain it did not imply anything very elevated. Provided, then, that there was a demand for culture, and that culture was not actually deleterious, I concluded I was justified in making my living by supplying that demand—and that all others in my position (dons, schoolmasters, professional authors, critics, reviewers) were similarly justified; especially if, like me, they had few or no talents for any other career—if their 'vocation' to a cultural profession consisted in the brute fact of not being fit for anything else.

2. But is culture even harmless? It certainly can be harmful and often is. If a Christian found himself in the position of one inaugurating a new society *in vacuo* he might well decide not to introduce something whose abuse is so easy and whose use is, at any rate, not necessary. But that is not our position. The abuse of culture is already there, and will continue whether Christians cease to be cultured or not. It is therefore probably better that the ranks of the 'culture-sellers' should include some Christians—as an antidote. It may even be the duty of some Christians to be culture-sellers. Not that I have yet said anything to show that even the lawful use of culture stands very high. The lawful use might be no more than innocent pleasure; but if the abuse is common, the task of resisting that abuse might be not only lawful but obligatory. Thus people in my position might be said to

be 'working the thing which is good' in a stronger sense than that reached in the last paragraph.

In order to avoid misunderstanding, I must add that when I speak of 'resisting the abuse of culture' I do not mean that a Christian should take money for supplying one thing (culture) and use the opportunity thus gained to supply a quite different thing (homiletics and apologetics). That is stealing. The mere presence of Christians in the ranks of the culture-sellers will inevitably provide an antidote.

It will be seen that I have now reached something very like the Gregorian view of culture as a weapon. Can I now go a step further and find any intrinsic goodness in culture for its own sake?

3. When I ask what culture has done to me personally, the most obviously true answer is that it has given me quite an enormous amount of pleasure. I have no doubt at all that pleasure is in itself a good and pain in itself an evil; if not, then the whole Christian tradition about heaven and hell and the passion of our Lord seems to have no meaning. Pleasure, then, is good; a 'sinful' pleasure means a good offered, and accepted, under conditions which involve a breach of the moral law. The pleasures of culture are not intrinsically bound up with such conditions—though of course they can very easily be so enjoyed as to involve them. Often, as Newman saw, they are an excellent diversion from guilty pleasures. We may, therefore, enjoy them ourselves, and lawfully, even charitably, teach others to enjoy them.

This view gives us some ease, though it would go a very little way towards satisfying the editors of *Scrutiny*. We should, indeed, be justified in propagating good taste on the ground that cultured pleasure in the arts is more varied, intense, and lasting, than vulgar or 'popular' pleasure.[1] But we should not regard it as meritorious. In fact, much as we should differ from Bentham about value in general, we should have to be Benthamites on the issue between pushpin and poetry.

4. It was noticed above that the values assumed in literature were seldom those of Christianity. Some of the principal values actually implicit in European literature were described as (a) honour, (b) sexual love, (c) material prosperity, (d) pantheistic contemplation of nature, (e) *Sehnsucht* awakened by the past, the

[1] If this is true, as I should gladly believe but have never seen proved.

21

remote, or the (imagined) supernatural, (f) liberation of impulses. These were called 'sub-Christian'. This is a term of disapproval if we are comparing them with Christian values: but if we take 'sub-Christian' to mean 'immediately sub-Christian' (i.e. the highest level of merely natural value lying immediately below the lowest level of spiritual value) it may be a term of relative approval. Some of the six values I have enumerated may be sub-Christian in this (relatively) good sense. For (c) and (f) I can make no defence; whenever they are accepted by the reader with anything more than a 'willing suspension of disbelief' they must make him worse. But the other four are all two-edged. I may symbolize what I think of them all by the aphorism 'Any road out of Jerusalem must also be a road into Jerusalem.' Thus:

(a) To the perfected Christian the ideal of honour is simply a temptation. His courage has a better root, and, being learned in Gethsemane, may have no honour about it. But to the man coming up from below, the ideal of knighthood may prove a schoolmaster to the ideal of martyrdom. Galahad is the *son* of Launcelot.

(b) The road described by Dante and Patmore is a dangerous one. But mere animalism, however disguised as 'honesty', 'frankness', or the like, is not dangerous, but fatal. And not all are qualified to be, even in sentiment, eunuchs for the Kingdom's sake. For some souls romantic love also has proved a schoolmaster.[1]

(d) There is an easy transition from Theism to Pantheism; but there is also a blessed transition in the other direction. For some souls I believe, for my own I remember, Wordsworthian contemplation can be the first and lowest form of recognition that there is something outside ourselves which demands reverence. To return to Pantheistic errors about the nature of this something would, for a Christian, be very bad. But once again, for 'the man coming up from below' the Wordsworthian experience is an advance. Even if he goes no further he has escaped the worst arrogance of materialism: if he goes on he will be converted.

(e) The dangers of romantic *Sehnsucht* are very great. Eroticism and even occultism lie in wait for it. On this subject I can only give my own experience for what it is worth. When we are first converted I suppose we think mostly of our recent sins; but

[1] See Charles Williams, *He Came Down from Heaven.*

as we go on, more and more of the terrible past comes under review. In this process I have not (or not yet) reached a point at which I can honestly repent of my early experiences of romantic *Sehnsucht*. That they were occasions to much that I do repent, is clear; but I still cannot help thinking that this was my abuse of them, and that the experiences themselves contained, from the very first, a wholly good element. Without them my conversion would have been more difficult.[1]

I have dwelt chiefly on certain kinds of literature, not because I think them the only elements in culture that have this value as schoolmasters, but because I know them best; and on literature rather than art and knowledge for the same reason. My general case may be stated in Ricardian terms—that culture is a storehouse of the best (sub-Christian) values. These values are in themselves of the soul, not the spirit. But God created the soul. Its values may be expected, therefore, to contain some reflection or antepast of the spiritual values. They will save no man. They resemble the re-generate life only as affection resembles charity, or honour resembles virtue, or the moon the sun. But though 'like is not the same', it is better than unlike. Imitation may pass into initiation. For some it is a good beginning. For others it is not; culture is not everyone's road into Jerusalem, and for some it is a road out.

There is another way in which it may predispose to conversion. The difficulty of converting an uneducated man nowadays lies in his complacency. Popularized science, the conventions or 'unconventions' of his immediate circle, party programmes, etc., enclose him in a tiny windowless universe which he mistakes for the only possible universe. There are no distant horizons, no mysteries. He thinks everything has been settled. A cultured person, on the other hand, is almost compelled to be aware that reality is very odd and that the ultimate truth, whatever it may be, *must* have the characteristics of strangeness—*must* be something that would seem remote and fantastic to the uncultured. Thus some obstacles to faith have been removed already.

[1] I am quite ready to describe *Sehnsucht* as 'spilled religion', provided it is not forgotten that the spilled drops may be full of blessing to the unconverted man who licks them up, and therefore begins to search for the cup whence they were spilled. For the drops will be taken by some whose stomachs are not yet sound enough for the full draught.

On these grounds I conclude that culture has a distinct part to play in bringing certain souls to Christ. Not all souls—there is a shorter, and safer, way which has always been followed by thousands of simple affectional natures who begin, where we hope to end, with devotion to the person of Christ.

Has it any part to play in the life of the converted? I think so, and in two ways. (a) If all the cultural values, on the way up to Christianity, were dim antepasts and ectypes of the truth, we can recognize them as such still. And since we must rest and play, where can we do so better than here—in the suburbs of Jerusalem? It is lawful to rest our eyes in moonlight—especially now that we know where it comes from, that it is only sunlight at second hand. (b) Whether the purely contemplative life is, or is not, desirable for any, it is certainly not the vocation of all. Most men must glorify God by doing to His glory something which is not *per se* an act of glorifying but which becomes so by being offered. If, as I now hope, cultural activities are innocent and even useful, then they also (like the sweeping of the room in Herbert's poem) can be done to the Lord. The work of a charwoman and the work of a poet become spiritual in the same way and on the same condition. There must be no return to the Arnoldian or Ricardian view. Let us stop giving ourselves airs.

If it is argued that the 'sensitivity' which Brother Every desires is something different from my 'culture' or 'good taste', I must reply that I have chosen those words as the most general terms for something which is differently conceived in every age—'wit', 'correctness', 'imagination' and (now) 'sensitivity'. These names, of course, record real changes of opinion about it. But if it were contended that the latest conception is so different from all its predecessors that we now have a radically new situation—that while 'wit' was not necessary for a seventeenth-century Christian, 'sensitivity' is necessary for a twentieth-century Christian—I should find this very hard to believe. 'Sensitivity' is a potentiality, therefore neutral. It can no more be an end to Christians than 'experience'. If Philippians i, 9, is quoted against me, I reply that delicate discriminations are there traced to charity, not to critical experience of books. Every virtue is a *habitus*—i.e. a *good* stock response. Dr Richards very candidly recognizes this when he speaks of people 'hag-ridden by their vices *or their virtues*' (*op. cit.,*

p. 52, italics mine). But we want to be so ridden. I do not want a sensitivity which will show me how different each temptation to lust or cowardice is from the last, how unique, how unamenable to general rules. A stock response is precisely what I need to acquire. Moral theologians, I believe, tell us to fly at sight from temptations to faith or chastity. If that is not (in Dr Richards' words) a 'stock', 'stereotyped', 'conventional' response, I do not know what is. In fact, the new ideal of 'sensitivity' seems to me to present culture to Christians in a somewhat less favourable light than its predecessors. Sidney's poetics would be better. The whole school of critical thought which descends from Dr Richards bears such deep marks of its anti-Christian origins that I question if it can ever be baptized.

II

To the Editor of *Theology*.

Sir,

Mr Bethell's main position is so important that I hope you will allow me at some future date to deal with it in a full-length argument. For the moment, therefore, I will only say: (1) That I made no reference to his previous paper for the worst of reasons and the best of causes—namely, that I had forgotten it. For this negligence I ask his pardon. On looking back at the relevant number of *Theology*, I see from marginalia in my own hand that I must have read his contribution with great interest; for my forgetfulness I can only plead that a great many things have happened to us all since then. I am distressed that Mr Bethell should suppose himself deliberately slighted. I intended no disrespect to him. (2) That my position 'logically implies ... total depravity' I deny simply. How any logician could derive the proposition 'Human nature is totally depraved' from the proposition 'Cultural activities do not in themselves improve our spiritual condition', I cannot understand. Even if I had said (which I did not), 'Man's aesthetic nature is totally depraved,' no one could infer 'Man's whole nature is totally depraved' without a glaring transference from *secundum quid* to *simpliciter*. I put it to Mr Bethell that he has used 'logically implies' to mean 'may without gross uncharity rouse the suspicion of'—and that he ought not to use words that way.

To Mr Carritt I reply that my argument assumed the divinity of Christ, the truth of the creeds, and the authority of the Christian tradition, because I was writing in an Anglican periodical. That is why Dominical and patristic sayings have for me more than an antiquarian interest. But though my attribution of authority to Christ or the Fathers may depend on premises which Mr Carritt does not accept, my belief that it is proper to combine my own reasonings with the witness of authority has a different ground, prior to any decision on the question, 'Who is authoritative?' One of the things my reason tells me is that I ought to check the results of my own thinking by the opinions of the wise. I go to authority because reason sends me to it—just as Mr. Carritt, after adding up a column of figures, might ask a friend, known to be a good calculator, to check it for him, and might distrust his own result if his friend got a different one.

I said that culture was a storehouse of the best sub-Christian *values*, not the best sub-Christian *virtues*. I meant by this that culture recorded man's striving for those ends which, though not the true end of man (the fruition of God), have nevertheless some degree of similarity to it, and are not so grossly inadequate to the nature of man as, say, physical pleasure, or money. This similarity, of course, while making it less evil to rest in them, makes the danger of resting in them greater and more subtle.

The salvation of souls is a means to the glorifying of God because only saved souls can duly glorify Him. The thing to which, on my view, culture must be subordinated, is not (though it includes) moral virtue, but the conscious direction of all will and desire to a transcendental Person in whom I believe all values to reside, and the reference to Him in every thought and act. Since that Person 'loves righteousness' this total surrender to Him involves Mr Carritt's 'conscientiousness'. It would therefore be impossible to 'glorify God by doing what we thought wrong'. Doing what we think right, on the other hand, is not the same as glorifying God. I fully agree with Mr Carritt that *a priori* we might expect the production of whatever is 'good' to be one of our duties. If God had never spoken to man, we should be justified in basing the conduct of life wholly on such *a priori* grounds.

Those who think God has spoken will naturally listen to what He has to say about the where, how, to what extent, and in what spirit any 'good' is to be pursued. This does not mean that our own 'conscience' is simply negated. On the contrary, just as reason sends me to authority, so conscience sends me to obedience: for one of the things my conscience tells me is that if there exists an absolutely wise and good Person (Aristotle's φρόνιμος raised to the nth) I owe Him obedience, specially when that Person, as the ground of my existence, has a kind of paternal claim on me, and, as a benefactor, has a claim on my gratitude. What would happen if there were an absolute clash between God's will and my own conscience—i.e. if *either* God could be bad *or* I were an incurable moral idiot—I naturally do not know, any more than Mr Carritt knows what would happen if he found absolutely demonstrative evidence for two contradictory propositions.

I mentioned Hooker, not because he simply denied that Scripture contains all things necessary, but because he advanced a proof that it cannot—which proof, I supposed, most readers of *Theology* would remember. 'Text-hunting' is, of course, 'Puritanical', but also scholastic, patristic, apostolic, and Dominical. To *that* kind of charge I venture, presuming on an indulgence which Mr Carritt has extended to me for nearly twenty years, to reply with homely saws: as that an old trout can't be caught by tickling, and they know a trick worth two of that where I come from. Puritan, quotha!

Yours faithfully,
C. S. LEWIS

III

PEACE PROPOSALS FOR BROTHER EVERY AND MR BETHELL

I BELIEVE there is little real disagreement between my critics (Brother Every and Mr Bethell) and myself. Mr Carritt, who does not accept the Christian premises, must here be left out of account, though with all the respect and affection I feel for my old tutor and friend.

The conclusion I reached in *Theology*, March, 1940, was that culture, though not in itself meritorious, was innocent and pleasant, might be a vocation for some, was helpful in bringing certain souls to Christ, and could be pursued to the glory of God. I do not see that Brother Every and Mr Bethell really want me to go beyond this position.

The argument of Mr Bethell's paper in *Theology*, July, 1939 (excluding its historical section, which does not here concern us), was that the deepest, and often unconscious, beliefs of a writer were implicit in his work, even in what might seem the minor details of its style, and that, unless we were Croceans, such beliefs must be taken into account in estimating the value of that work. In *Theology*, May, 1940, Mr Bethell reaffirmed this doctrine, with the addition that the latent beliefs in much modern fiction were naturalistic, and that we needed trained critics to put Christian readers on their guard against this pervasive influence.

Brother Every, in *Theology*, September, 1940, maintained that our tastes are symptomatic of our real standards of value, which may differ from our professed standards; and that we needed trained critics to show us the real latent standards in literature— in fact 'to teach us how to read'.

I cannot see that my own doctrine and those of my critics come into direct contradiction at any point. My fear was lest excellence in reading and writing were being elevated into a spiritual value, into something meritorious *per se*; just as other things excellent and wholesome in themselves, like conjugal love (in the sense of *eros*) or physical cleanliness, have, at some times and in some circles been confused with virtue itself or esteemed necessary parts of it. But it now appears that my critics never intended to make any such claim. Bad Taste for them is not itself spiritual evil but the symptom which betrays, or the 'carrier' which circulates, spiritual evil. And the spiritual evil thus betrayed or carried turns out not to be any specifically cultural or literary kind of evil, but false beliefs or standards—that is, intellectual error or moral baseness; and as I never intended to deny that error and baseness were evils nor the literature could imply and carry them, I think that all three of us may shake hands and say we are agreed. I do not mean to suggest that my critics have *merely* restated a platitude which neither I nor anyone else ever disputed. The value of their contribution lies in their insistence that the real beliefs may differ from the professed and may lurk in the turn of a phrase or the choice of an epithet; with the result that many preferences which seem to the ignorant to be simply 'matters of taste' are visible to the trained critic as choices between good and evil, or truth and error. And I fully admit that this important point had been neglected in my essay of March, 1940. Now that it has been made, I heartily accept it. I think this is agreement.

But to test the depth of agreement I would like my critics to consider the following positions. By agreement I mean only agreement in our doctrines. Differences of temper and emphasis between Christian critics are inevitable and probably desirable.

1. Is it the function of the 'trained critic' to discover the latent beliefs and standards in a book, or to pass judgement on them when discovered, or both? I think Brother Every confines the critic's function to discovery. About Mr Bethell I am not so sure. When he says (*Theology*, May, 1940, p. 360) that we need a minority of trained critics to 'lay bare the false values of contemporary culture' this might mean two things: (*a*) 'To expose the falsity of the values of contemporary culture'; (*b*) 'To reveal what the values of contemoprary culture actually are—and, by the way, I personally think those values false.' It is necessary to clear this up before we know what is meant by a 'trained critic'. Trained in what? A man who has had a literary training may be an expert in disengaging the beliefs and values latent in literature; but the judgement on those beliefs and values (that is, the judgement on all possible human thoughts and moralities) belongs either to a quite different set of experts (theologians, philosophers, casuists, scientists) or else not to experts at all but to the unspecialized 'good and wise man', the φρόνιμος. Now I for my part have no objection to our doing both when we criticize, but I think it very important to keep the two operations distinct. In the discovery of the latent belief we have had a special training, and speak as experts; in the judgement of the beliefs, once they have been discovered, we humbly hope that we are being trained, like everyone else, by reason and ripening experience, under the guidance of the Holy Ghost, as long as we live, but we speak on them simply as men, on a level with all our even-Christians, and indeed with less authority than any illiterate man who happens to be older, wiser, and purer, than we. To transfer to these judgements any specialist

authority which may belong to us as 'trained critics' is charlatanism, if the attempt is conscious, and confusion if it is not. If Brother Every (see *Theology*, September, 1940, p. 161) condemns a book because of 'English Liberal' implications he is really saying two things: (*a*) This book has English Liberal implications; (*b*) English Liberalism is an evil. The first he utters with authority because he is a trained critic. In the second, he may be right or he may be wrong; but he speaks with no more authority than any other man. Failure to observe this distinction may turn literary criticism into a sort of stalking horse from behind which a man may shoot all his personal opinions on any and every subject, without ever really arguing in their defence and under cover of a quite irrelevant specialist training in literature. I do not accuse Brother Every of this. But a glance at any modern review will show that it is an ever-present danger.

2. In *Theology*, May, 1940 (p. 359), Mr Bethell speaks of 'some form of biological or economic naturalism' as the unconscious attitude in most popular fiction of today, and cites, as straws that show the wind, the popularity of 'urges' and 'overmastering passions'. Now, fortunately, I agree with Mr Bethell in thinking naturalism an erroneous philosophy: and I am ready to grant, for the purposes of argument, that those who talk about 'urges' do so because they are unconsciously naturalistic. But when all this has been granted, can we honestly say that the *whole* of our dislike of 'urges' is explained, without remainder, by our disagreement with naturalism? Surely not. Surely we object to that way of writing for another reason *as well*—because it is so worn, so facile, so obviously attempting to be impressive, so associated in our minds with dullness and pomposity.[1] In other words, there are two elements in our reaction. One is the detection of an attitude in the writer which, as instructed Christians and amateur philosophers, we disapprove; the other is really, and strictly, an affair of taste. Now these, again, require to be kept distinct. Being fallen creatures we tend to resent offences against our taste, at least as much as, or even more than, offences against our conscience or

---

[1] Pomp is at times a literary virtue. Pomposity (the unsuccessful attempt at pomp) may, of course, spring from an evil (pride); it may also be the maladroit effort of a humble writer to 'rise' to a subject which he honestly feels to be great.

reason; and we would dearly like to be able—if only we can find any plausible argument for doing so—to inflict upon the man whose writing (perhaps for reasons utterly unconnected with good and evil) has afflicted us like a bad smell, the same kind of condemnation which we can inflict on him who has uttered the false and the evil. The tendency is easily observed among children; friendship wavers when you discover that a hitherto trusted playmate actually *likes* prunes. But even for adults it is 'sweet, sweet, sweet poison' to feel able to imply 'thus saith the Lord' at the end of every expression of our pet aversions. To avoid this horrible danger we must perpetually try to distinguish, however closely they get entwined both by the subtle nature of the facts and by the secret importunity of our passions, those attitudes in a writer which we can honestly and confidently condemn as real evils, and those qualities in his writing which simply annoy and offend us as men of taste. This is difficult, because the latter are often so much more obvious and provoke such a very violent response. The only safe course seems to me to be this: to reserve our condemnation of attitudes for attitudes universally acknowledged to be bad by the Christian conscience speaking in agreement with Scripture and ecumenical tradition. A bad book is to be deemed a real evil in so far as it can be shown to prompt to sensuality, or pride, or murder, or to conflict with the doctrine of Divine Providence, or the like. The other dyslogistic terms dear to critics (vulgar, derivative, cheap, precious, academic, affected, bourgeois, Victorian, Georgian, 'literary', etc.) had better be kept strictly on the taste side of the account. In discovering what attitudes are present you can be as subtle as you like. But in your theological and ethical condemnation (as distinct from your dislike of the taste) you had better be very un-subtle. You had better reserve it for plain mortal sins, and plain atheism and heresy. For our passions are always urging us in the opposite direction, and if we are not careful criticism may become a mere excuse for taking revenge on books whose smell we dislike by erecting our temperamental antipathies into pseudo-moral judgements.

3. In practical life a certain amount of 'reading between the lines' is necessary: if we took every letter and every remark simply at its face value we should soon find ourselves in difficulties. On the other hand, most of us have known people with whom 'reading

between the lines' became such a mania that they overlooked the obvious truth of every situation and lived in the perpetual discovery of mares' nests; and doctors tell us of a form of lunacy in which the simplest remark uttered in the patient's presence becomes to him evidence of a conspiracy and the very furniture of his cell takes on an infinitely sinister significance. Will my critics admit that the subtle and difficult task of digging out the latent beliefs and values, however necessary, is attended with some danger of our neglecting the obvious and surface facts about a book, whose importance, even if less than that of the latent facts, is certainly much higher than zero? Suppose two books A and B. Suppose it can be truly said of A: 'The very style of this book reveals great sensitivity and honesty, and a readiness for total commitments; excellent raw material for sanctity if ever the author were converted.' And suppose it can be truly said of B: 'The very style of this book betrays a woolly, compromising state of mind, knee-deep entangled in the materialistic values which the author thinks he has rejected.' But might it not also be true to say of book A, 'Despite its excellent latent implications, its ostensible purpose (which will corrupt thousands of readers) is the continued glorification of mortal sin'; and of B, 'Despite its dreadful latent materialism, it does set courage and fidelity before the reader in an attractive light, and thousands of readers will be edified (though much less edified than they suppose) by reading it'? And is there not a danger of this second truth being neglected? We want the abstruse knowledge *in addition to* the obvious: not *instead of* it.

4. It is clear that the simple and ignorant are least able to resist, by reason, the influence of latent evil in the books they read. But is it not also true that this is often balanced by a kind of protection which comes to them through ignorance itself? I base this on three grounds: (*a*) Adults often disquiet themselves about the effect of a work upon children—for example, the effect of the bad elements in *Peter Pan*, such as the desire not to grow up or the sentimentalities about Wendy. But if I may trust my own memory, childhood simply does not receive these things. It rightly wants and enjoys the flying, the Indians, and the pirates (not to mention the pleasure of being in a theatre at all), and just accepts the rest as part of the meaningless 'roughage' which occurs in all books and

plays; for at that age we never expect any work of art to be interesting all through. (When I began writing stories in exercise books I tried to put off all the things I really wanted to write about till at least the second page—I thought it wouldn't be like a real grown-up book if it became interesting at once.) (*b*) I often find expressions in my pupils' essays which seem to me to imply a great deal of latent error and evil. Now, since it would, in any case, be latent, one does not expect them to own up to it when challenged. But one does expect that a process of exploration would discover the mental atmosphere to which the expression belonged. But in my experience exploration often produces a conviction that it had, in my pupils' minds, no evil associations, because it had no associations at all. They just thought it was the ordinary way of translating thought into what they suppose to be 'literary English'. Thousands of people are no more corrupted by the implications of 'urges', 'dynamism', and 'progressive' than they are edified by the implications of 'secular', 'charity', and 'Platonic'.[1] The same process of attrition which empties good language of its virtue does, after all, empty bad language of much of its vice.[2] (*c*) If one speaks to an uneducated man about some of the worst features in a film or a book, does he not often reply unconcernedly, 'Ah . . . they always got to bring a bit of that into a film,' or, 'I reckon they put that in to wind it up like'? And does this not mean that he is aware, even to excess, of the difference between art and life? He *expects* a certain amount of meaningless nonsense—which expectation, though very regrettable from the cultural point of view, largely protects him from the consequences of which we, in our sophisticated naivety, are afraid.

5. Finally, I agree with Brother Every that our leisure, even our play, is a matter of serious concern. There is no neutral ground in the universe: every square inch, every split second, is claimed by God and counterclaimed by Satan. But will Brother

[1] For example, God forbid that when Mr Bethell (May, 1940, p. 361) uses 'old-fashioned' as a dyslogistic term we should immediately conclude that he really had the garage or dressmaking philosophy (Madam would like the *latest* model) which his words suggest. We know it slipped out by a sort of accident, for which *veniam petimus damusque vicissim.*

[2] This applies also to 'bad language' in the popular sense, obscenity or profanity. The custom of such language has its origin in sin, but to the individual speaker it may be mere meaningless noise.

Every agree in acknowledging a real difficulty about merely recreational reading (I do not include all reading under this head), as about games? I mean that they are serious, and yet, to do them at all, we must somehow do them as if they were not. It is a serious matter to choose wholesome recreations: but they would no longer be recreations if we pursued them seriously. When Mr Bethell speaks of the critic's 'working hours' (May, 1940, p. 360) I hope he means his hours of criticism, not his hours of reading. For a great deal (not all) of our literature was made to be read lightly, for entertainment. If we do not read it, in a sense, 'for fun' and with our feet on the fender, we are not using it as it was meant to be used, and all our criticism of it will be pure illusion. For you cannot judge any artefact except by using it as it was intended. It is no good judging a butter-knife by seeing whether it will saw logs. Much bad criticism, indeed, results from the efforts of critics to get a work-time result out of something that never aimed at producing more than pleasure. There is a real problem here, and I do not see my way through it. But I should be disappointed if my critics denied the existence of the problem.

If any real disagreement remains between us, I anticipate that it will be about my third point—about the distinction there drawn between the real spiritual evil carried or betrayed in a book and its mere faults of taste. And on this subject I confess that my critics can present me with a very puzzling dilemma. They can ask me whether the statement, 'This is tawdry writing', is an objective statement describing something bad in a book and capable of being true or false, or whether it is merely a statement about the speaker's own feelings—different in form, but fundamentally the same, as the proposition 'I don't like oysters.' If I choose the latter, then most criticism becomes purely subjective—which I don't want. If I choose the former then they can ask me, 'What are these qualities in a book which you admit to be in some sense good and bad but which, you keep on warning us, are not "really" or "spiritually" good and bad? Is there a kind of good which is not good? Is there any good that is not pleasing to God or any bad which is not hateful to Him?' And if you press me along these lines I end in doubts. But I will not get rid of those doubts by falsifying the little light I already have. That little light seems to compel me to say that there are two kinds of good and bad. The first, such as virtue and vice or love and hatred, besides being good or bad themselves make the possessor good or bad. The second do not. They include such things as physical beauty or ugliness, the possession or lack of a sense of humour, strength or weakness, pleasure or pain. But the two most relevant for us are the two I mentioned at the beginning of this essay, conjugal *eros* (as distinct from *agape*, which, of course, is a good of the first class) and physical cleanliness. Surely we have all met people who said, indeed, that the latter was *next* to godliness, but whose unconscious attitude made it a *part* of godliness, and no small part? And surely we agree that any good of this second class, however good on its own level, becomes an enemy when it thus assumes demonic pretensions and erects itself into a quasi-spiritual value. As M. de Rougemont has recently told us, the conjugal *eros* 'ceases to be a devil only when it ceases to be a god'. My whole contention is that in literature, in addition to the spiritual good and evil which it carries, there is also a good and evil of this second class, a properly cultural or literary good and evil, which must not be allowed to masquerade as good and evil of the first class. And I shall feel really happy about all the minor differences between my critics and me when I find in them some recognition of this danger—some admission that they and I, and all of the like education, are daily tempted to a kind of idolatry.

I am not pretending to know how this baffling phenomenon— the two kinds or levels of good and evil—is to be fitted into a consistent philosophy of values. But it is one thing to be unable to explain a phenomenon, another to ignore it. And I admit that all of these lower goods ought to be encouraged, that, as pedagogues, it is our duty to try to make our pupils happy and beautiful, to give them cleanly habits and good taste; and the discharge of that duty is, of course, a good of the first class. I will admit, too, that evils of this second class are often the result and symptom of real spiritual evil; dirty finger-nails, a sluggish liver, boredom, and a bad English style, may often in a given case result from disobedience, laziness, arrogance, or intemperance. But they may also result from poverty or other misfortune. They may even result from virtue. The man's ears may be unwashed behind or his English style borrowed from the jargon of the daily press, because he has given to good works the time and energy which others use to acquire elegant habits or good language. Gregory the Great, I believe vaunted the barbarity of his style. Our Lord ate with unwashed hands.

I am stating, not solving, a problem. If my critics want to continue the discussion I think they can do so most usefully by taking it right away from literature and the arts to some other of these mysterious 'lower goods'—where, probably, all our minds will work more coolly. I should welcome an essay from Brother Every or Mr Bethell on conjugal *eros* or personal cleanliness. My dilemma about literature is that I admit bad taste to be, in some sense, 'a bad thing', but do not think it *per se* 'evil'. My critics will probably say the same of physical dirt. If we could thrash the problem out on the neutral ground of clean and dirty fingers, we might return to the battlefield of literature with new lights.

I hope it is now unnecessary to point out that in denying 'taste' to be a spiritual value, I am not for a moment suggesting, as Mr Bethell thought (May, 1940, p. 357), that it comes 'under God's arbitrary condemnation'. I enjoyed my breakfast this morning, and I think that was a good thing and do not think it was condemned by God. But I do not think myself a good man for enjoying it. The distinction does not seem to me a very fine one.

RELIGION: REALITY OR SUBSTITUTE?

Hebrews X, 1. 'The Law having a shadow of good things to come.'

We are all quite familiar with this idea, that the old Jewish priesthood was a mere symbol and that Christianity is the reality which it symbolized. It is important, however, to notice what an astonishing, even impudent, claim it must have seemed as long as the temple at Jerusalem was still standing. In the temple you saw real sacrifice being offered—real animals really had their throats cut and their actual flesh and blood were used in the ritual; in Christian assemblies a ceremony with wine and bits of bread was conducted. It must have been all but impossible to resist the conviction that the Jewish service was the reality and the Christian one a mere substitute—wine is so obviously a substitute for blood and bread for flesh! Yet the Christians had the audacity to maintain that it was the other way round—that their innocuous little ritual meal in private houses was the real sacrifice and that all the slaughtering, incense, music, and shouting in the temple was merely the shadow.

In considering this we touch upon the very central region where all doubts about our religion live. Things do look so very much as if our whole faith were a substitute for the real well-being we have failed to achieve on earth. It seems so very likely that our rejection of the World is only the disappointed fox's attempt to convince himself that unattainable grapes are sour. After all, we do not usually think much about the next world till our hopes in this have been pretty well flattened out—and when they are revived we not infrequently abandon our religion. And does not all that talk of celestial love come chiefly from monks and nuns, starved celibates consoling themselves with a compensatory hallucination? And the worship of the Christ child—does it not also come to us from centuries of lonely old maids? There is no good ignoring these disquieting thoughts. Let us admit from

37

the outset that the psychologists have a good *prima facie* case. The theory that our religion is a substitute has a great deal of plausibility.

Faced with this, the first thing I do is to try to find out what I know about substitutes, and the realities for which they are substituted, in general. And I find that I don't know so much as I thought I did. Until I considered the matter I had a sort of impression that one could recognize the difference by mere inspection if one was really honest—that the substitute would somehow betray itself by the mere taste, would ring false. And this impression was, in fact, one of the sources from which the doubts I mentioned were drawing their strength. What made it seem so likely that religion was a substitute was not any general philosophical argument about the existence of God, but rather the experienced fact that for the most of us at most times the spiritual life *tasted* so thin, or insipid, compared with the natural. And I thought that was just what a substitute might be expected to taste like. But after reflection, I discovered that this was not only not an obvious truth but was even contradicted by some of my own experience.

I once knew two bad boys who smoked secretly and stole their father's tobacco. Their father had cigarettes, which he really smoked himself, and cigars—a great many cigars—which he kept for visitors. The boys liked cigarettes very much better than cigars. But every now and then there would come a day when their father had let his supply of cigarettes get so low that the boys thought the theft of even one or two would inevitably be detected. On such days they took cigars instead; and one of them would say to the other: 'I'm afraid we'll have to put up with cigars today', and the other would reply: 'Well, I suppose a cigar is better than nothing.' This is not a fable I'm inventing, but a historical fact that I can vouch for. And here, surely, we have a very good instance of the value to be attached to anyone's first hasty ideas about a reality and a substitute. To these children, a cigar was simply an inferior substitute for a cigarette, a *pis-aller*. And, of course, the boys, at that stage, were quite right about their own feelings: but they would have become ludicrously wrong if they had therefore inferred that cigars, in their own nature, were merely a kind of makeshift cigarette. On that question their own childish experience offered them no evidence: they had to learn the answer from quite different sources, or else to wait until their palates were grown up. And may I add the important moral of the story? One of these boys has been permanently punished by a life-long inability to appreciate cigars.

Here is another example. When I was a boy, gramophone records were not nearly so good as they are now. In the old recording of an orchestral piece you could hardly hear the separate instrument at all, but only a single undifferentiated sound. That was the sort of music I grew up on. And when, at a somewhat later age, I began to hear real orchestras, I was actually disappointed with them, just because you didn't get that single sound. What one got in a concert room seemed to me to lack the unity I had grown to expect, to be not an orchestra but merely a number of individual musicians on the same platform. In fact, I felt it 'wasn't the Real Thing'. This is an even better example than the former one. For a gramophone record is precisely a substitute, and an orchestra the reality. But owing to my musical miseducation the reality appeared to be a substitute and the substitute a reality.

'Substitutes' suggest wartime feeding. Well, there too I have an example. During the last war, as at present, we had to eat margarine instead of butter. When I began doing so I couldn't tell the difference between them. For the first week or so, I would have said, 'you may call the margarine a substitute if you like, but it is actually just as good as the real thing'. But by the end of the war I could never again have mistaken one for the other and I never wanted to see margarine again. This is different from the previous examples because here I started knowing which, in fact, was the substitute. But the point is that mere immediate taste did not at first confirm this bit of knowledge. It was only after long experience that the margarine revealed itself to my senses as the inferior.

But enough of my own experiences. I will turn to a better man. to Milton, and to that scene which I used to think the most grotesque, but now think one of the most profound, in *Paradise Lost*. I mean the part where Eve, a few minutes after her creation, sees herself in a pool of water, and falls in love with her own reflection. Then God makes her look up, and she sees Adam. But the interesting point is that the first sight of Adam is a disappointment; he is a much less immediately attractive object than herself. Being divinely guided, Eve gets over this difficult *pons asinorum* and lives to learn that being in love with Adam is more inexhaustible, more fruitful, and even better fun, than being in love with herself. But if she had been a sinner, like ourselves, she would not have made the transition so easily; she also would have passed through the stage of finding the real, external lover a second best. Indeed the region from which this example is drawn illustrates my theme better than almost any other. To the pervert, normal love, when it does not appear simply repulsive, appears at best a mere milk and water substitute for that ghastly world of impossible fantasies which have become to him the 'real thing'. But every department of life furnishes us with examples. The ears that are delighted with jazz cannot quite believe that 'classical music' is anything but a sort of 'vegetarian jazz' (to quote my friend Barfield), and great literature seems to vulgar taste at first a pale reflection of the 'thrillers' or 'triangle dramas' which it prefers.

From all this I want to draw the following conclusion. Introspection is of no use at all in deciding which of two experiences is a substitute or a second best. At a certain stage all those sensations which we should expect to find accompanying the proper satisfaction of a fundamental need will actually accompany the substitute, and *vice versa*. And I want to insist that if we are once convinced of this principle, we should then hold it quite unflinchingly from this moment to the end of our lives. When a witness has once been proved unreliable, turn him out of the court. It is mere waste of time to go sneaking back to his evidence and thinking 'After all' and 'He *did* say'. If immediate feeling has shown itself quite worthless in this matter, then let us never listen to immediate feeling again. If our criterion between a real, and a substituted, satisfaction must be sought somewhere else, then in God's name, seek it somewhere else.

When I say 'somewhere else' I am not yet speaking of Faith or a supernatural gift. What I mean can be shown by an example. If those two bad boys had really wanted to find out whether their view of cigars and cigarettes were correct, there were various things they might have done. They might have asked a grown-up, who would have told them that cigars were actually regarded as the greater luxury of the two, and thus had their error corrected by authority. Or they might have found out by their own researches—that is by buying their smokes instead of stealing them —that cigars were more expensive than cigarettes and thence inferred that they could not in reality be a mere substitute for them. This would have been correction by reason. Finally, they might have practised obedience, honesty, and truthfulness and waited till an age at which they were allowed to smoke—in which case they would have arrived at a more reasonable view about these two ways of preparing tobacco by experience. Authority, reason, experience; on these three, mixed in varying proportions all our knowledge depends. The authority of many wise men in many different times and places forbids me to regard the spiritual world as an illusion. My reason, showing me the apparently insoluble difficulties of materialism and proving that the hypothesis of a spiritual world covers far more of the facts with far fewer assumptions, forbids me again. My experience even of such feeble attempts as I have made to live the spiritual life does not lead to the results which the pursuit of an illusion ordinarily leads to, and therefore forbids me yet again. I am not now saying that no one's reason and no one's experience produce different results. I am only trying to put the whole problem the right way round, to make it clear that the value given to the testimony of any feeling must depend on our whole philosophy, not our whole philosophy on a feeling. If those who deny the spiritual world prove their case on general grounds, then, indeed, it will follow that our apparently spiritual experiences *must* be an illusion; but equally, if we are right, it will follow that they are the prime reality and that our natural experiences are a second best. And let us note that whichever view we embrace, mere feeling will continue to assault our conviction. Just as the Christian has his moments when the clamour of this visible and audible world is so persistent and the whisper of the spiritual world so faint that faith and reason can hardly stick to their guns, so, as I well remember, the atheist too has his moments of shuddering misgiving, of an all but irresistible suspicion that old tales may after all be true, that something or someone from outside may at any moment break into his neat, explicable, mechanical universe. Believe in God and you will have to face hours when it seems *obvious* that this material world is the only reality: disbelieve in Him and you must face hours when this material world seems to shout at you that it is *not* all. No conviction, religious or irreligious, will, of itself, end once and for all this fifth-columnist in the soul. Only the practice of Faith resulting in the habit of Faith will gradually do that.

Have we now got to a position from which we can talk about Faith without being misunderstood? For in general we are shy of speaking plain about Faith as a virtue. It looks so like praising an intention to believe what you want to believe in the face of evidence to the contrary: the American in the old story defined Faith as 'the power of believing what we know to be untrue'. Now I define Faith as the power of continuing to believe what we once honestly thought to be true until cogent reasons for honestly changing our minds are brought before us. The difficulty of such continuing to believe is constantly ignored or misunderstood in discussions of this subject. It is always assumed that the difficulties of faith are intellectual difficulties, that a man who has once accepted a certain proposition will automatically go on believing it till real grounds for disbelief occur. Nothing could be more superficial. How many of the freshmen who come up to Oxford from religious homes and lose their Christianity in the first year have been honestly *argued* out of it? How many of our own sudden temporary losses of faith have a rational basis which would stand examination for a moment? I don't know how it is with others, but I find that mere change of scene always has a tendency to decrease my faith at first—God is less credible when I pray in a hotel bedroom than when I am in College. The society of unbelievers makes Faith harder even when they are people whose opinions, on any other subject, are known to be worthless.

These irrational fluctuations in belief are not peculiar to religious belief. They are happening about all our beliefs all day long. Haven't you noticed it with our thoughts about the war? Some days, of course, there is really good or really bad news, which gives us rational grounds for increased optimism or pessimism. But everyone must have experienced days in which we are caught up in a great wave of confidence or down into a trough of anxiety though there are no new grounds either for the one or the other. Of course, once the mood is on us, we *find* reasons soon enough. We say that we've been 'thinking it over': but it is pretty plain that the mood has created the reasons and not *vice versa*. But there are examples closer to the Christian problem even than these. There are things, say in learning to swim or to climb, which look dangerous and aren't. Your instructor tells you it's safe. You have

42

good reason from past experience to trust him. Perhaps you can even see for yourself, by your own reason, that it is safe. But the crucial question is, will you be able to go on believing this when you actually see the cliff edge below you or actually feel yourself unsupported in the water? You will have no *rational* grounds for disbelieving. It is your senses and your imagination that are going to attack belief. Here, as in the New Testament, the conflict is not between faith and reason but between faith and sight. We can face things which we *know* to be dangerous if they don't look or sound too dangerous; our real trouble is often with things we *know* to be safe but which look dreadful. Our faith in Christ wavers not so much when real arguments come against it as when it *looks* improbable—when the whole world takes on that desolate *look* which really tells us much more about the state of our passions and even our digestion than about reality.

When we exhort people to Faith as a virtue, to the settled intention of continuing to believe certain things, we are not exhorting them to fight against reason. The intention of continuing to believe is required because, though Reason is divine, human reasoners are not. When once passion takes part in the game, the human reason, unassisted by Grace, has about as much chance of retaining its hold on truths already gained as a snow-flake has of retaining its consistency in the mouth of a blast furnace. The sort of arguments against Christianity which our reason can be persuaded to accept at the moment of yielding to temptation are often preposterous. Reason may win truths; without Faith she will retain them just so long as Satan pleases. There is nothing we cannot be made to believe or disbelieve. If we wish to be rational, not now and then, but constantly, we must pray for the gift of Faith, for the power to go on believing not in the teeth of reason but in the teeth of lust and terror and jealousy and boredom and indifference that which reason, authority, or experience, or all three, have once delivered to us for truth. And the answer to that prayer will, perhaps, surprise us when it comes. For I am not sure, after all, whether one of the causes of our weak faith is not a secret wish that our faith should *not* be very strong. Is there some reservation in our minds? Some fear of what it might be like if our religion became *quite* real? I hope not. God help us all, and forgive us.

43

ON ETHICS

It is often asserted in modern England that the world must return to Christian ethics in order to preserve civilization, or even in order to save the human species from destruction. It is sometimes asserted in reply that Christian ethics have been the greatest obstacle to human progress and that we must take care never to return to a bondage from which we have at last so fortunately escaped. I will not weary you with a repetition of the common arguments by which either view could be supported. My task is a different one. Though I am myself a Christian, and even a dogmatic Christian untinged with Modernist reservations and committed to supernaturalism in its full rigour, I find myself quite unable to take my place beside the upholders of the first view. The whole debate between those who demand and those who deprecate a return to Christian ethics, seems to me to involve presuppositions which I cannot allow. The question between the contending parties has been wrongly put.

I must begin by distinguishing the senses in which we may speak of ethical systems and of the differences between them. We may, on the one hand, mean by an ethical system a body of ethical injunctions. In this sense, when we speak of Stoical Ethics we mean the system which strongly commends suicide (under certain conditions) and enjoins Apathy in the technical sense, the extinction of the emotions: when we speak of Aristotelian ethics we mean the system which finds in Virtuous Pride or Magnanimity the virtue that presupposes and includes all other virtues; when we speak of Christian ethics we mean the system that commands humility, forgiveness, and (in certain circumstances) martyrdom. The differences, from this point of view, are differences of content. But we also sometimes speak of Ethical Systems when we mean systematic analyses and explanations of our moral experience. Thus the expression 'Kantian Ethics' signifies not primarily a body of commands—Kant did not differ remarkably from other men on the content of ethics—but the doctrine of the

Categorical Imperative. From this point of view Stoical Ethics is the system which defines moral behaviour by conformity to Nature, or the whole, or Providence—terms almost interchangeable in Stoical thought: Aristotelian ethics is the system of eudaemonism: Christian ethics, the system which, whether by exalting Faith above Works, by asserting that love fulfils the Law, or by demanding Regeneration, makes duty a self-transcending concept and endeavours to escape from the region of mere morality.

It would of course be naïve to suppose that there is no profound connection between an ethical system in the one sense and an ethical system in the other. The philosopher's or theologian's theory of ethics arises out of the practical ethics he already holds and attempts to obey; and again, the theory, once formed, reacts on his judgement of what ought to be done. That is a truth in no danger of being neglected by an age so steeped in historicism[1] as ours. We are, if anything, too deeply imbued with the sense of period, too eager to trace a common spirit in the ethical practice and ethical theory, in the economics, institutions, art, dress and language of a society. It must, however, also be insisted that Ethical Systems in the one sense do not differ in a direct ratio to the difference of Ethical Systems in another. The number of actions about whose ethical quality a Stoic, an Aristotelian, a Thomist, a Kantian, and a Utilitarian would agree is, after all very large. The very act of studying diverse ethical theories, as theories, exaggerates the practical differences between them. While we are studying them from that point of view we naturally and, for that purpose, rightly seize on the marginal case where the theoretical difference goes with a contradiction between the injunctions, because it is the *experimentum crucis*. But the exaggeration useful in one inquiry must not be carried over into other inquiries.

When modern writers urge us to return, or not to return, to Christian Ethics, I presume they mean Christian Ethics in our first sense: a body of injunctions, not a theory as to the origin, sanctions, or ultimate significance, of those injunctions. If they do not mean that, then they should not talk about a return to Christian Ethics but simply about a return to Christianity. I will at any rate assume that in this debate Christian Ethics means a body of injunctions.

[1 See Lewis's essay on 'Historicism', pp. 100ff.]

And now my difficulties begin. A debate about the desirability of adopting Christian Ethics seems to proceed upon two presuppositions. (1) That Christian Ethics is one among several alternative bodies of injunctions, so clearly distinct from one another that the whole future of our species in this planet depends on our choice between them. (2) That we to whom the disputants address their pleadings, are for the moment standing outside all these systems in a sort of ethical vacuum, ready to enter whichever of them is most convincingly recommended to us. And it does not appear to me that either presupposition corresponds at all closely or sensitively to the reality.

Consider with me for a moment the first presupposition. Did Christian Ethics really enter the world as a novelty, a new, peculiar set of commands, to which a man could be in the strict sense *converted*? I say converted to the practical ethics: he could of course be converted to the Christian faith, he could accept, not only as a novelty, but as a transcendent novelty, a mystery hidden from all eternity, the deity and resurrection of Jesus, the Atonement, the forgiveness of sins. But these novelties themselves set a rigid limit to the novelty we can assume in the ethical injunctions. The convert accepted forgiveness of sins. But of sins against what Law? Some new law promulgated by the Christians? But that is nonsensical. It would be the mockery of a tyrant to forgive a man for doing what had never been forbidden until the very moment at which the forgiveness was announced. The idea (at least in its grossest and most popular form) that Christianity brought a new ethical code into the world is a grave error. If it had done so, then we should have to conclude that all who first preached it wholly misunderstood their own message: for all of them, its Founder, His precursor, His apostles, came demanding repentance and offering forgiveness, a demand and an offer both meaningless except on the assumption of a moral law already known and already broken.

It is far from my intention to deny that we find in Christian ethics a deepening, an internalization, a few changes of emphasis, in the moral code. But only serious ignorance of Jewish and Pagan culture would lead anyone to the conclusion that it is a radically new thing. Essentially, Christianity is not the promulgation of a moral discovery. It is addressed only to penitents, only to those who admit their disobedience to the known moral law. It offers forgiveness for having broken, and supernatural help towards keeping, that law, and by so doing re-affirms it. A Christian who understands his own religion laughs when unbelievers expect to trouble him by the assertion that Jesus uttered no command which had not been anticipated by the Rabbis—few, indeed, which cannot be paralleled in classical, ancient Egyptian, Ninevite, Babylonian, or Chinese texts.[1] We have long recognized that truth with rejoicing. Our faith is not pinned on a crank.

The second presupposition—that of an ethical vacuum in which we stand deciding what code we will adopt—is not quite so easily dealt with, but I believe it to be, in the long run, equally misleading. Of course, historically or chronologically, a man need not be supposed to stand outside all ethical codes at the moment when you exhort him to adopt Christian ethics. A man who is attending one lecturer or one physician may be advised to exchange him for another. But he cannot come to a decision without first reaching a moment of indecision. There must be a point at which he feels himself attached to neither and weighs their rival merits. Adherence to either is inconsistent with choice. In the same way, the demand that we should reassume, or refrain from re-assuming, the Christian code of ethics, invites us to enter a state in which we shall be unattached.

I am not, of course, denying that some men at some times can be in an ethical vacuum, adhering to no Ethical System. But most of those who are in that state are by no means engaged in deciding what system they shall adopt, for such men do not often propose to adopt any. They are more often concerned with getting out of gaols or asylums. Our question is not about them. Our question is whether the sort of men who urge us to return (or not to return) to Christian Ethics, or the sort of men who listen to such appeals, can enter the ethical vacuum which seems to be involved in the

[1 Readers will have already recognized themes in this paper which recall the main argument of Lewis's *Abolition of Man* (Oxford, 1943; Bles, 1946)—a book which is, in my opinion, an all but indispensable introduction to the entire *corpus* of Lewisiana. Though I am unable to establish a date for this paper, my guess is that it anticipates the *Abolition* by a year or so.

On the similarities in various ethical systems, see his 'Illustrations of the *Tao*' (= The Way, or the Natural Law) which forms the Appendix to *The Abolition of Man*.]

very conception of choosing an ethical code. And the best way of answering this question is (as sometimes happens) by asking another first. Supposing we can enter the vacuum and view all Ethical Systems from the outside, what sort of motives can we then expect to find for entering any one of them?

One thing is immediately clear. We can have no *ethical* motives for adopting any of these systems. It cannot, while we are in the vacuum, be our duty to emerge from it. An act of duty is an act of obedience to the moral law. But by definition we are standing outside all codes of moral law. A man with no ethical allegiance can have no ethical motive for adopting one. If he had, it would prove that he was not really in the vacuum at all. How then does it come about that men who talk as if we could stand outside all moralities and choose among them as a woman chooses a hat, nevertheless exhort us (and often in passionate tones) to make some one particular choice? They have a ready answer. Almost invariably they recommend some code of ethics on the ground that it, and it alone, will preserve civilization, or the human race. What they seldom tell us is whether the preservation of the human race is itself a duty or whether they expect us to aim at it on some other ground.

Now if it is a duty, then clearly those who exhort us to it are not themselves really in a moral vacuum, and do not seriously believe that we are in a moral vacuum. At the very least they accept, and count on our accepting, one moral injunction. Their moral code is, admittedly, singularly poor in content. Its solitary command, compared with the richly articulated codes of Aristotle, Confucius, or Aquinas, suggests that it is a mere residuum; as the arts of certain savages suggest that they are the last vestige of a vanished civilization. But there is a profound difference between having a fanatical and narrow morality and having no morality at all. If they were really in a moral vacuum, whence could they have derived the idea of even a single duty?

In order to evade the difficulty, it may be suggested that the preservation of our species is not a moral imperative but an end prescribed by Instinct. To this I reply, firstly, that it is very doubtful whether there is such an instinct; and secondly, that if there were, it would not do the work which those who invoke instinct in this context demand of it.

48

Have we in fact such an instinct? We must here be careful about the meaning of the word. In English the word *instinct* is often loosely used for what ought rather to be called appetite: thus we speak of the sexual instinct. *Instinct* in this sense means an impulse which appears in consciousness as desire, and whose fulfilment is marked by pleasure. That we have no instinct (in this sense) to preserve our species, seems to me self-evident. Desire is directed to the concrete—this woman, this plate of soup, this glass of beer: but the preservation of the species is a high abstraction which does not even enter the mind of unreflective people, and affects even cultured minds most at those times when they are least instinctive. But instinct is also, and more properly, used to mean Behaviour as if from knowledge. Thus certain insects carry out complicated actions which have in fact the result that their eggs are hatched and their larvae nourished: and since (rightly or wrongly) we refuse to attribute conscious design and foreknowledge to the agent we say that it has acted 'by instinct'. What that means on the subjective side, how the matter appears, if it appears at all, to the insect, I suppose we do not know. To say, in this sense, that we have an instinct to preserve the human race, would be to say that we find ourselves compelled, we know not how, to perform acts which in fact (though that was not our purpose) tend to its preservation. This seems very unlikely. What are these acts? And if they exist, what is the purpose of urging us to preserve the race by adopting (or avoiding) Christian Ethics? Had not the job better be left to instinct?

Yet again, *Instinct* may be used to denote these strong impulses which are, like the appetites, hard to deny though they are not, like the appetites, directed to concrete physical pleasure. And this, I think, is what people really mean when they speak of an instinct to preserve the human race. They mean that we have a natural, unreflective, spontaneous impulse to do this, as we have to preserve our own offspring. And here we are thrown back on the debatable evidence of introspection. I do not find that I have this impulse, and I do not see evidence that other men have it. Do not misunderstand me. I would not be thought a monster. I acknowledge the preservation of man as an end to which my own preservation and happiness are subordinate; what I deny is that that end has been prescribed to me by a powerful, spontaneous impulse.

The truth seems to me to be that we have such an impulse to preserve our children and grandchildren, an impulse which progressively weakens as we carry our minds further and further into the abyss of future generations, and which, if left to its own spontaneous strength, soon dies out altogether. Let me ask anyone in this audience who is a father whether he has a spontaneous impulse to sacrifice his own son for the sake of the human species in general. I am not asking whether he would so sacrifice his son. I am asking whether, if he did so, he would be obeying a spontaneous impulse. Will not every father among you reply that if this sacrifice were demanded of him and if he made it, he would do so not in obedience to a natural impulse but in hard-won defiance of it? Such an act, no less than the immolation of oneself, would be a triumph over nature.

But let us leave that difficulty on one side. Let us suppose, for purposes of argument, that there really is an 'instinct' (in whatever sense) to preserve civilization, or the human race. Our instincts are obviously in conflict. The satisfaction of one demands the denial of another. And obviously the instinct, if there is one, to preserve humanity, is the one of all others whose satisfaction is likely to entail the greatest frustration of my remaining instincts. My hunger and thirst, my sexual desires, my family affections, are all going to be interfered with. And remember, we are still supposed to be in the vacuum, outside all ethical systems. On what conceivable ground, in an ethical void, on the assumption that the preservation of the species is not a moral but a merely instinctive end, can I be asked to gratify my instinct for the preservation of the species by adopting a moral code? Why should this instinct be preferred to all my others? It is certainly not my strongest. Even if it were, why should I not fight against it as a dipsomaniac is exhorted to fight against his tyrannous desire? Why do my advisers assume from the very outset, without argument, that this instinct should be given a dictatorship in my soul? Let us not be cheated with words. It is no use to say that this is the deepest, or highest, or most fundamental, or noblest of my instincts. Such words either mean that it is my strongest instinct (which is false and would be no reason for obeying it even if it were true) or else conceal a surreptitious re-introduction of the ethical.

And in fact the ethical has been re-introduced. Or, more

accurately, it has never really been banished. The moral vacuum was from the outset a mere figment. Those who expect us to adopt a moral code as a means to the preservation of the species have themselves already a moral code and tacitly assume that we have one too. Their starting point is a purely moral maxim *That humanity ought to be preserved*. The introduction of instinct is futile. If you do not arrange our instincts in a hierarchy of comparative dignity, it is idle to tell us to obey instinct, for the instincts are at war. If you do, then you are arranging them in obedience to a moral principle, passing an ethical judgement upon them. If instinct is your only standard, no instinct is to be preferred to another: for each of them will claim to be gratified at the expense of all the rest. Those who urge us to choose a moral code are already moralists. We may throw away the preposterous picture of a wholly unethical man confronted with a series of alternative codes and making his free choice between them. Nothing of the kind occurs. When a man is wholly unethical he does not choose between ethical codes. And those who say they are choosing between ethical codes are already assuming a code.

What, then, shall we say of the maxim which turns out to be present from the beginning—*That humanity ought to be preserved*? Where do we get it from? Or, to be more concrete, where do I get it from? Certainly, I can point to no moment in time at which I first embraced it. It is, so far as I can make out, a late and abstract generalization from all the moral teaching I have ever had. If I now wanted to find authority for it, I should have no need to appeal to my own religion. I could point to the confession of the righteous soul in the Egyptian *Book of the Dead*—'I have not slain men.' I could find in the Babylonian Hymn that he who meditates oppression will find his house overturned. I would find, nearer home in the Elder Edda that 'Man is man's delight.' I would find in Confucius that the people should first be multiplied, then enriched, and then instructed. If I wanted the spirit of all these precepts generalized I could find in Locke that 'by the fundamental law of Nature Man is to be preserved as much as possible'.

Thus from my point of view there is no particular mystery about this maxim. It is what I have been taught, explicitly and implicitly, by my nurse, my parents, my religion, by sages or poets from every culture of which I have any knowledge. To reach this maxim I have no need to choose one ethical code among many and excogitate impossible motives for adopting it. The difficulty would be to find codes that contradict it. And when I had found them they would turn out to be, not radically different things, but codes in which the same principle is for some reason restricted or truncated: in which the preservation and perfection of Man shrinks to that of the tribe, the class, or the family, or the nation. They could all be reached by mere subtraction from what seems to be the general code: they differ from it not as ox from man but as dwarf from man.

Thus far as concerns myself. But where do those others get it from, those others who claimed to be standing outside all ethical codes? Surely there is no doubt about the answer. They found it where I found it. They hold it by inheritance and training from the general (if not strictly universal) human tradition. They would never have reached their solitary injunction if they had really begun in an ethical vacuum. They have trusted the general human tradition at least to the extent of taking over from it one maxim.

But of course in that tradition this maxim did not stand alone. I found beside it many other injunctions: special duties to parents and elders, special duties to my wife and child, duties of good faith and veracity, duties to the weak, the poor and the desolate (these latter not confined, as some think, to the Judaic–Christian texts). And for me, again, there is no difficulty. I accept all these commands, all on the same authority. But there is surely a great difficulty for those who retain one and desire to drop the rest? And now we come to the heart of our subject.

There are many people in the modern world who offer us, as they say, new moralities. But as we have just seen there can be no moral motive for entering a new morality unless that motive is borrowed from the traditional morality, which is neither Christian nor Pagan, neither Eastern nor Western, neither ancient nor modern, but general. The question then arises as to the reasonableness of taking one maxim and rejecting the rest. If the remaining maxims have no authority, what is the authority of the one you have selected to retain? If it has authority, why have the others no authority? Thus a scientific Humanist may urge us to get rid of what he might call our inherited *Taboo* morality and realize that the total exploitation of nature for the comfort and security of posterity is the sole end. His system clashes with mine, say, at the point where he demands the compulsory euthanasia of the aged or the unfit. But the duty of caring for posterity, on which he bases his whole system, has no other source than that same tradition which bids me honour my parents and do no murder (a prohibition I find in the *Voluspa* as well as in the Decalogue). If, as he would have me believe, I have been misled by the tradition when it taught me my duty to my parents, how do I know it has not misled me equally in prescribing a duty to posterity? Again, we may have a fanatical Nationalist who tells me to throw away my antiquated scruples about universal justice and benevolence and adopt a system in which nothing but the wealth and power of my own country matters. But the difficulty is the same. I learned of a special duty to my own country in the same place where I also learned of a general duty to men as such. If the tradition was wrong about the one duty, on what ground does the Nationalist ask me to believe that it was right about the other? The Communist is in the same position. I may well agree with him that exploitation is an evil and that those who do the work should reap the reward. But I only believe this because I accept certain traditional notions of justice. When he goes on to attack justice as part of my *bourgeois* ideology, he takes away the very ground on which I can reasonably be asked to accept his new communistic code.

Let us very clearly understand that, in a certain sense, it is no more possible to invent a new ethics than to place a new sun in the sky. Some precept from traditional morality always has to be assumed. We never start from a *tabula rasa*: if we did, we should end, ethically speaking, with a *tabula rasa*. New moralities can only be contractions or expansions of something already given. And all the specifically modern attempts at new moralities are contractions. They proceed by retaining some traditional precepts and rejecting others: but the only real authority behind those which they retain is the very same authority which they flout in rejecting others. Of course this inconsistency is concealed; usually, as we have seen, by a refusal to recognize the precepts that are retained as moral precepts at all.

But many other causes contribute to the concealment. As in the

life of the individual so in that of a community, particular circumstances set a temporary excess of value on some one end. When we
are in love, the beloved, when we are ill, health, when we are poor,
money, when we are frightened, safety, seems the only thing worth
having. Hence he who speaks to a class, a nation, or a culture, in
the grip of some passion, will not find it difficult to insinuate into
their minds the fatal idea of some one finite good which is worth
achieving at all costs, and building an eccentric ethical system on
that foundation. It is, of course, no genuinely new system. Whatever the chosen goal may be, the idea that I should seek it for my
class or culture or nation at the expense of my own personal
satisfaction has no authority save that which it derives from traditional morality. But in the emotion of the moment this is overlooked.

Added to this, may we not recognize in modern thought a very
serious exaggeration of the ethical differences between different
cultures? The conception which dominates our thought is en-
shrined in the word *ideologies*, in so far as that word suggests that
the whole moral and philosophical outlook of a people can be
explained without remainder in terms of their method of production, their economic organization, and their geographical position.
On that view, of course, differences, and differences to any extent,
are to be expected between ideologies as between languages and
costumes. But is this what we actually find? Much anthropology
seems at first to encourage us to answer Yes. But if I may venture
on an opinion in a field where I am by no means an expert, I
would suggest that the appearance is somewhat illusory. It seems
to me to result from a concentration on those very elements in
each culture which are most variable (sexual practice and religious
ritual) and also from a concentration on the savage. I have even
found a tendency in some thinkers to treat the savage as the normal or archetypal man. But surely he is the exceptional man. It
may indeed be true that we were all savages once, as it is certainly
true that we were all babies once. But we do not treat as normal
man the imbecile who remains in adult life what we all were
(intellectually) in the cradle. The savage has had as many generations of ancestors as the civilized man: he is the man who, in the
same number of centuries, either has not learned or has forgotten,
what the rest of the human race know. I do not see why we should

attach much significance to the diversity and eccentricity (them-selves often exaggerated) of savage codes. And if we turn to civi-lized man, I claim that we shall find far fewer differences of ethical injunction than is now popularly believed. In triumphant mono-tony the same indispensable platitudes will meet us in culture after culture. The idea that any of the new moralities now offered us would be simply one more addition to a variety already almost infinite, is not in accordance with the facts. We are not really justified in speaking of different moralities as we speak of different languages or different religions.

You will not suspect me of trying to reintroduce in its full Stoical or medieval rigour the doctrine of Natural Law. Still less am I claiming as the source of this substantial ethical agreement anything like Intuition or Innate Ideas. Nor, Theist though I am, do I here put forward any surreptitious argument for Theism. My aim is more timid. It is even negative. I deny that we have any choice to make between clearly differentiated ethical systems. I deny that we have any power to make a new ethical system. I assert that wherever and whenever ethical discussion begins we find already before us an ethical code whose validity has to be assumed before we can even criticize it. For no ethical attack on any of the traditional precepts can be made except on the ground of some other traditional precept. You can attack the concept of justice because it interferes with the feeding of the masses, but you have taken the duty of feeding the masses from the world-wide code. You may exalt patriotism at the expense of mercy; but it was the old code that told you to love your country. You may vivisect your grandfather in order to deliver your grandchildren from cancer: but, take away traditional morality, and why should you bother about your grandchildren?

Out of these negatives, there springs a positive. Men say 'How are we to act, what are we to teach our children, now that we are no longer Christians?' You see, gentlemen, how I would answer that question. You are deceived in thinking that the morality of your father was based on Christianity. On the contrary, Christi-anity presupposed it. That morality stands exactly where it did; its basis has not been withdrawn for, in a sense, it never had a basis. The ultimate ethical injunctions have always been premisses, never conclusions. Kant was perfectly right on that point at least:

the imperative is categorical. Unless the ethical is assumed from the outset, no argument will bring you to it.

In thus recalling men to traditional morality I am not of course maintaining that it will provide an answer to every particular moral problem with which we may be confronted. M. Sartre seems to me to be the victim of a curious misunderstanding when he rejects the conception of general moral rules on the ground that such rules may fail to apply clearly to all concrete problems of conduct. Who could ever have supposed that by accepting a moral code we should be delivered from all questions of casuistry? Obviously it is moral codes that create questions of casuistry, just as the rules of chess create chess problems. The man without a moral code, like the animal, is free from moral problems. The man who has not learned to count is free from mathematical problems. A man asleep is free from all problems. Within the framework of general human ethics problems will, of course, arise and will sometimes be solved wrongly. This possibility of error is simply the symptom that we are awake, not asleep, that we are men, not beasts or gods. If I were pressing on you a panacea, if I were recommending traditional ethics as a means to some end, I might be tempted to promise you the infallibility which I actually deny. But that, you see, is not my position. I send you back to your nurse and your father, to all the poets and sages and law givers, because, in a sense, I hold that you are already there whether you recognize it or not: that there is really no ethical alternative: that those who urge us to adopt new moralities are only offering us the mutilated or expurgated text of a book which we already possess in the original manuscript. They all wish us to depend on them instead of on that original, and then to deprive us of our full humanity. Their activity is in the long run always directed against our freedom.

DE FUTILITATE

When I was asked to address you, Sir Henry Tizard suggested that the problem of futility was likely to be present to many of your minds. It would have been raised by the disappointment of all those hopes with which the last war closed and the uneasy feeling that the results of the present war may prove equally disappointing. And if I remember rightly he also hinted that the feeling of futility might go even deeper. The eschatological hopes which supported our more remote, and Christian ancestors, and the secular hopes which supported the Revolutionaries or even the Liberals of the last century, have both rather faded out. There is a certain vacuity left: a widespread question as to what all this hustling and crowded life is *about*, or whether indeed it is about anything.

Now in one way I am the worst person in the world to address you on this subject. Perhaps because I had a not very happy boyhood, or perhaps because of some peculiarity in my glands, I am too familiar with the idea of futility to feel the shock of it so sharply as a good speaker on the subject ought to. Early in this war a labouring man who was doing a midnight Home Guard Patrol with another educated man and myself, discovered from our conversation that we did not expect that this war would end wars, or, in general, that human misery would ever be abolished. I shall never forget that man standing still there in the moonlight for at least a whole minute, as this entirely novel idea sank in and at last breaking out 'Then what's the good of the ruddy world going on?' What astonished me—for I was as much astonished as the workman—was the fact that this misgiving was wholly new to him. How, I wondered, could a man have reached the middle forties without ever before doubting whether there *was* any good in the ruddy world going on? Such security was to me unimaginable. I can understand a man coming in the end, and after prolonged consideration, to the view that existence is not futile. But how any man could have taken it for granted beat me, and beats me still. And if there is anyone present whose fear of futility is based solely on such local and temporary facts as the war or the almost equally threatening prospect of the next peace, I must ask him to bear with me while I suggest that we have to face the possibility of a much deeper and more radical futility: one which, if it exists at all, is wholly incurable.

This cosmic futility is concealed from the masses by popular Evolutionism. Speaking to a scientifically trained audience I need not labour the point that popular Evolutionism is something quite different from Evolution as the biologists understand it. Biological Evolution is a theory about how organisms change. Some of these changes have made organisms, judged by human standards, 'better'—more flexible, stronger, more conscious. The majority of the changes have not done so. As J. B. S. Haldane says, in evolution progress is the exception and degeneration the rule. Popular Evolutionism ignores this. For it, 'Evolution' simply means 'improvement'. And it is not confined to organisms, but applied also to moral qualities, institutions, arts, intelligence and the like. There is thus lodged in popular thought the conception that improvement is, somehow, a cosmic law: a conception to which the sciences give no support at all. There is no general tendency even for organisms to improve. There is no evidence that the mental and moral capacities of the human race have been increased since man became man. And there is certainly no tendency for the universe as a whole to move in any direction which we should call 'good'. On the contrary, Evolution—even if it were what the mass of the people suppose it to be—is only (by astronomical and physical standards) an inconspicuous foreground detail in the picture. The huge background is filled by quite different principles: entropy, degradation, disorganization. Everything suggests that organic life is going to be a very short and unimportant episode in the history of the universe. We have often heard individuals console themselves for their individual troubles by saying: 'It will be all the same 100 years hence.' But you can do the like about our troubles as a species. Whatever we do it is all going to be the same in a few hundred million years hence. Organic life is only a lightning flash in cosmic history. In the long run, nothing will come of it.

Now do not misunderstand me. I am not for one moment trying to suggest that this long-term futility provides any ground for diminishing our efforts to make human life, while it lasts, less painful and less unfair than it has been up to date. The fact that the ship is sinking is no reason for allowing her to be a floating hell while she still floats. Indeed, there is a certain fine irony in the idea of keeping the ship very punctiliously in good order up to the very moment at which she goes down. If the universe is shameless and idiotic, that is no reason why we should imitate it. Well brought up people have always regarded the tumbril and the scaffold as places for one's best clothes and best manners. Such, at least, was my first reaction to the picture of the futile cosmos. And I am not, in the first instance, suggesting that that picture should be allowed to make any difference to our practice. But it must make a difference to our thoughts and feelings.

Now it seems to me that there are three lines, and three only, which one can take about this futility. In the first place, you can simply 'take it'. You can become a consistent pessimist, as Lord Russell was when he wrote *The Worship of a Free Man*, and base your whole life on what he called 'a firm foundation of unshakable despair'. You will feed yourself on the Wessex novels and *The Shropshire Lad* and Lucretius: and a very manly, impressive figure you may contrive to be. In the second place you can deny the picture of the universe which the scientists paint. There are various ways of doing this. You might become a Western Idealist or an Oriental Pantheist. In either case you would maintain that the material universe was, in the last resort, not quite real. It is a kind of mirage produced by our senses and forms of thought: Reality is to be sought elsewhere. Or you might say— as Jews, Mohammedans and Christians do, that though Nature is real as far as she goes, still there are other realities, and that by bringing them in you alter the picture so much that it is no longer a picture of futility. Or thirdly, one could accept the scientific picture and try to do something about the futility. I mean, instead of criticizing the universe we may criticize our own feeling about the universe, and try to show that our sense of futility is unreasonable or improper or irrelevant. I imagine this third procedure will seem to you, at any rate to begin with, the most promising. Let us explore it.

I think the most damaging criticism we can level against our own feeling of cosmic futility is this: 'Futility' is the opposite of 'utility'. A machine or plan is futile when it does not serve the purpose for which it was devised. In calling the universe futile, therefore, we are really applying to it a means-and-end pattern of thought: treating it as if it were a thing manufactured and manufactured for some purpose. In calling it futile we are only expressing our naïve surprise at the discovery that basic reality does not possess the characteristics of a human artefact—a thing made by men to serve the purposes of men—and the demand that it should may be regarded as preposterous: it is rather like complaining that a tree is futile because the branches don't happen to come just where we want them for climbing it—or even a stone because it doesn't happen to be edible.

This point of view certainly seems, at first, to have all the bracing shock of common sense, and I certainly believe that no philosophy which does not contain this view as at least one of its elements is at all likely to be true. But taken by itself it will turn out to be rather too simple.

If we push it to its logical conclusion we shall arrive at something like this. The proper way of stating the facts is not to say that the universe is futile, but that the universe has produced an animal, namely man, which can make tools. The long habit of making tools has engendered in him another habit—that of thinking in terms of means and ends. This habit becomes so deeply engrained that even when the creature is not engaged in tool-making it continues to use this pattern of thought—to 'project' it (as we say) upon reality as a whole. Hence arises the absurd practice of demanding that the universe should be 'good' or complaining that it is 'bad'. But such thoughts are *merely* human. They tell us nothing about the universe, they are merely a fact about Man—like his pigmentation or the shape of his lungs.

There is something attractive about this: but the question is how far we can go. Can we carry through to the end the view that human thought is *merely* human: that it is simply a zoological fact about *homo sapiens* that he thinks in a certain way: that it in no way reflects (though no doubt it results from) non-human or universal reality? The moment we ask this question, we receive a check. We are at this very point asking whether a certain view of human thought is true. And the view in question is just the view that human thought is *not* true, not a reflection of reality. And this view is itself a thought. In other words, we are asking 'Is the thought that no thoughts are true, itself true?' If we answer Yes, we contradict ourselves. For if all thoughts are untrue, then this thought is untrue.

There is therefore no question of a total scepticism about human thought. We are always prevented from accepting total scepticism because it can be formulated only by making a tacit exception in favour of the thought we are thinking at the moment —just as the man who warns the newcomer 'Don't trust anyone in this office' always expects you to trust him at that moment. Whatever happens, then, the most we can ever do is to decide that certain types of human thought are 'merely human' or subjective, and others not. However small the class, *some* class of thoughts must be regarded not as mere facts about the way human brains work, but as true insights, as the reflection of reality in human consciousness.

One popular distinction is between what is called scientific thought and other kinds of thought. It is widely believed that scientific thought does put us in touch with reality, whereas moral or metaphysical thought does not. On this view, when we say that the universe is a space-time continuum we are saying something about reality, whereas if we say that the universe is futile, or that men ought to have a living wage, we are only describing our own subjective feelings. That is why in modern stories of what the Americans call 'scientifictional' type—stories about unknown species who inhabit other planets or the depth of the sea— these creatures are usually pictured as being wholly devoid of our moral standards but as accepting our scientific standards. The implication is, of course, that scientific thought, being objective, will be the same for all creatures that can reason at all, whereas moral thought, being merely a subjective thing like one's taste in food, might be expected to vary from species to species.

But the distinction thus made between scientific and non-scientific thoughts will not easily bear the weight we are attempting to put on it. The cycle of scientific thought is from experiment to hypothesis and thence to verification and a new hypothesis. Experiment means sense-experiences specially arranged. Verification involves inference. 'If X existed, then, under conditions

Y, we should have the experience Z.' We then produce the conditions Y and Z appears. We thence infer the existence of X. Now it is clear that the only part of this process which assures us of any reality outside ourselves is precisely the inference 'If X, then Z', or conversely 'Since Z, therefore X'. The other parts of the process, namely hypothesis and experiment, cannot by themselves give us any assurance. The hypothesis is, admittedly, a mental construction—something, as they say, 'inside our own heads'. And the experiment is a state of our own consciousness. It is, say, a dial reading or a colour seen if you heat the fluid in the test tube. That is to say, it is a state of visual sensation. The apparatus used in the experiment is believed to exist outside our own minds only on the strength of an inference: it is inferred as the cause of our visual sensations. I am not at all suggesting that the inference is a bad one. I am not a subjective idealist and I fully believe that the distinction we make between an experiment in a dream and an experiment in a laboratory is a sound one. I am only pointing out that the material or external world in general is an inferred world and that therefore particular experiments, far from taking us out of the magic circle of inference into some supposed direct contact with reality, are themselves evidential only as parts of that great inference. The physical sciences, then, depend on the validity of logic just as much as metaphysics or mathematics. If popular thought feels 'science' to be different from all other kinds of knowledge because science is experimentally verifiable, popular thought is mistaken. Experimental verification is not a new kind of assurance coming in to supply the deficiencies of mere logic. We should therefore abandon the distinction between scientific and non-scientific thought. The proper distinction is between logical and non-logical thought. I mean, the proper distinction for our present purpose: that purpose being to find whether there is any class of thoughts which has objective value, which is not *merely* a fact about how the human cortex behaves. For that purpose we can make no distinction between science and other logical exercises of thought, for if logic is discredited science must go down along with it.

It therefore follows that all knowledge whatever depends on the validity of inference. If, in principle, the feeling of certainty we have when we say 'Because A is B therefore C must be D' is an illusion, if it reveals only how our cortex has to work and not how realities external to us must really be, then we can know nothing whatever. I say 'in principle' because, of course, through inattention or fatigue we often make false inferences and while we make them they feel as certain as the sound ones. But then they are always corrigible by further reasoning. That does not matter. What would matter would be if inference itself, even apart from accidental errors, were a merely subjective phenomenon.

Now let me go back a bit. We began by asking whether our feeling of futility could be set aside as a merely subjective and irrelevant result which the universe has produced in human brains. I postponed answering that question until we had attempted a larger one. I asked whether *in general* human thought could be set aside as irrelevant to the real universe and merely subjective. I now claim to have found the answer to this larger question. The answer is that at least one kind of thought—logical thought—cannot be subjective and irrelevant to the real universe: for unless thought is valid we have no reason to believe in the real universe. We reach our knowledge of the universe only by inference. The very object to which our thought is supposed to be irrelevant depends on the relevance of our thought. A universe whose only claim to be believed in rests on the validity of inference must not start telling us that inference is invalid. That would really be a bit too nonsensical. I conclude then that logic is a real insight into the way in which real things have to exist. In other words, the laws of thought are also the laws of things: of things in the remotest space and the remotest time.[1]

This admission seems to me completely unavoidable and it has very momentous consequences.

In the first place it rules out any materialistic account of thinking. We are compelled to admit between the thoughts of a terrestrial astronomer and the behaviour of matter several light-years away that particular relation which we call truth. But this

[1 Lewis's best and fullest treatment on the validity of human reasoning appears in the first six chapters of his book *Miracles: A Preliminary Study* (Bles, 1947), especially Chapter III, 'The Self-Contradiction of the Naturalist'. He later felt that he had in chapter III confused two senses of *irrational*; this chapter was rewritten and appears in its corrected form in the paper-backed edition of *Miracles* (Fontana Books, 1960).]

relation has no meaning at all if we try to make it exist between the matter of the star and the astronomer's brain, considered as a lump of matter. The brain may be in all sorts of relations to the star no doubt: it is in a spatial relation, and a time relation, and a quantitative relation. But to talk of one bit of matter as being true about another bit of matter seems to me to be nonsense. It might conceivably turn out to be the case that every atom in the universe thought, and thought truly, about every other. But that relation between any two atoms would be something quite distinct from the physical relations between them. In saying that thinking is not matter I am not suggesting that there is anything mysterious about it. In one sense, thinking is the simplest thing in the world. We do it all day long. We know what it is like far better than we know what matter is like. Thought is what we start from: the simple, intimate, immediate *datum*. Matter is the inferred thing, the mystery.

In the second place, to understand that logic must be valid is to see at once that this thing we all know, this thought, this mind, cannot in fact be really alien to the nature of the universe. Or, putting it the other way round, the nature of the universe cannot be really alien to Reason. We find that matter always obeys the same laws which our logic obeys. When logic says a thing must be so, Nature always agrees. No one can suppose that this can be due to a happy coincidence. A great many people think that it is due to the fact that Nature produced the mind. But on the assumption that Nature is herself mindless this provides no explanation. To be the result of a series of mindless events is one thing: to be a kind of plan or true account of the laws according to which those mindless events happened is quite another. Thus the Gulf Stream produces all sorts of results: for instance, the temperature of the Irish Sea. What it does not produce is maps of the Gulf Stream. But if logic, as we find it operative in our own minds, is really a result of mindless nature, then it is a result as improbable as that. The laws whereby logic obliges us to think turn out to be the laws according to which every event in space and time must happen. The man who thinks this an ordinary or probable result does not really understand. It is as if cabbages, in addition to resulting *from* the laws of botany also gave lectures in that subject: or as if, when I knocked out my pipe, the ashes arranged themselves into letters which read: 'We are the ashes of a knocked-out pipe.' But if the validity of knowledge cannot be explained in that way, and if perpetual happy coincidence throughout the whole of recorded time is out of the question, then surely we must seek the real explanation elsewhere.

I want to put this other explanation in the broadest possible terms and am anxious that you should not imagine I am trying to prove anything more, or more definite, than I really am. And perhaps the safest way of putting it is this: that we must give up talking about 'human reason'. In so far as thought is merely human, merely a characteristic of one particular biological species, it does not explain our knowledge. Where thought is strictly rational it must be, in some odd sense, not ours, but cosmic or super-cosmic. It must be something not shut up inside our heads but already 'out there'—in the universe or behind the universe: either as objective as material Nature or more objective still. Unless all that we take to be knowledge is an illusion, we must hold that in thinking we are not reading rationality into an irrational universe but responding to a rationality with which the universe has always been saturated. There are all sorts of different ways in which you can develop this position, either into an idealist metaphysic or a theology, into a theistic or a pantheistic or dualist theology. I am not tonight going to trace those possible developments, still less to defend the particular one which I myself accept. I am only going to consider what light this conception, in its most general form, throws on the question of futility.

As first sight it might seem to throw very little. The universe, as we have observed it, does not appear to be in any sense good as a whole, though it throws up some particular details which are very good indeed—strawberries and the sea and sunrise and the song of the birds. But these, quantitatively considered, are so brief and small compared with the huge tracts of empty space and the enormous masses of uninhabitable matter that we might well regard them as lucky accidents. We might therefore conclude that though the ultimate reality is logical it has no regard for values, or at any rate for the values we recognize. And so we could still accuse it of futility. But there is a real difficulty about accusing it of anything. An accusation always implies a standard. You call a man a bad golf player because you know what Bogey is. You call a boy's answer to a sum wrong because you know the right answer. You call a man cruel or idle because you have in mind a standard of kindness or diligence. And while you are making the accusation you have to accept the standard as a valid one. If you begin to doubt the standard you automatically doubt the cogency of your accusation. If you are sceptical about grammar you must be equally sceptical about your condemnation of bad grammar. If nothing is certainly right, then of course it follows that nothing is certainly wrong. And that is the snag about what I would call Heroic Pessimism—I mean the kind of Pessimism you get in Swinburne, Hardy and Shelley's *Prometheus* and which is magnificently summed up in Houseman's line 'Whatever brute and blackguard made the world'. Do not imagine that I lack sympathy with that kind of poetry: on the contrary, at one time of my life I tried very hard to write it—and, as far as quantity goes, I succeeded. I produced reams of it.[1] But there is a catch. If a Brute and Blackguard made the world, then he also made our minds. If he made our minds, he also made that very standard in them whereby we judge him to be a Brute and Blackguard. And how can we trust a standard which comes from such a brutal and blackguardly source? If we reject him, we ought also to reject all his works. But one of his works is this very moral standard by which we reject him. If we accept

[1 No doubt Lewis is referring to many of the poems in his first book, *Spirits in Bondage: A Cycle of Lyrics* (Heinemann, 1919) which he published under the pseudonym, Clive Hamilton. One of the best examples in the collection is the following lines from 'Ode for New Year's Day':

... Nature will not pity, nor the red God lend an ear.
Yet I too have been mad in the hour of bitter paining
And lifted up my voice to God, thinking that he could hear
The curse wherewith I cursed Him because the Good was dead.
But lo! I am grown wiser, knowing that our own hearts
Have made a phantom called the Good, while a few years have sped
Over a little planet ...

. . . . . .

Ah, sweet, if a man could cheat him! If you could flee away
Into some other country beyond the rosy West,
To hide in the deep forests and be for ever at rest
From the rankling hate of God and the outworn world's decay!]

this standard then we are really implying that he is not a Brute and Blackguard. If we reject it, then we have thrown away the only instrument by which we can condemn him. Heroic anti-theism thus has a contradiction in its centre. You must trust the universe in one respect even in order to condemn it in every other.

What happens to our sense of values is, in fact, exactly what happens to our logic. If it is a purely human sense of values— a biological by-product in a particular species with no relevance to reality—then we cannot, having once realized this, continue to use it as the ground for what are meant to be serious criticisms of the nature of things. Nor can we continue to attach any importance to the efforts we make towards realizing our ideas of value. A man cannot continue to make sacrifices for the good of posterity if he really believes that his concern for the good of posterity is simply an irrational subjective taste of his own on the same level with his fondness for pancakes or his dislike for spam. I am well aware that many whose philosophy involves this subjective view of values do in fact sometimes make great efforts for the cause of justice or freedom. But that is because they forget their philosophy. When they really get to work they think that justice is really good—objectively obligatory whether any one likes it or not: they remember their opposite philosophical belief only when they go back to the lecture room. Our sense that the universe is futile and our sense of a duty to make those parts of it we can reach less futile, both really imply a belief that it is not in fact futile at all: a belief that values are rooted in reality, outside ourselves, that the Reason in which the universe is saturated is also moral.

There remains, of course, the possibility that Its values are widely different from ours. And in some sense this must be so. The particular interpretation of the universe which I accept certainly represents them as differing from ours in many acutely distressing ways. But there are strict limits to the extent which we can allow to this admission.

Let us go back to the question of Logic. I have tried to show that you reach a self-contradiction if you say that logical inference is, in principle, invalid. On the other hand, nothing is more obvious than that we frequently make false inferences: from ignorance of some of the factors involved, from inattention, from inefficiencies in the system of symbols (linguistic or otherwise) which we are using, from the secret influence of our unconscious wishes or fears. We are therefore driven to combine a steadfast faith in inference as such with a wholesome scepticism about each particular instance of inference in the mind of a human thinker. As I have said, there is no such thing (strictly speaking) as *human reason*: but there is emphatically such a thing as human thought— in other words, the various specifically human conceptions of Reason, failures of complete rationality, which arise in a wishful and lazy human mind utilizing a tired human brain. The difference between acknowledging this and being sceptical about Reason itself, is enormous. For in the one case we should be saying that reality contradicts Reason, whereas now we are only saying that total Reason—cosmic or super-cosmic Reason—*corrects* human imperfections of Reason. Now correction is not the same as mere contradiction. When your false reasoning is corrected you 'see the mistakes': the true reasoning thus takes up into itself whatever was already rational in your original thought. You are not moved into a totally new world; you are given *more* and *purer* of what you already had in a small quantity and badly mixed with foreign elements. To say that Reason is objective is to say that all our false reasonings could in principle be corrected by more Reason. I have to add 'in principle' because, of course, the reasoning necessary to give us absolute truth about the whole universe might be (indeed, certainly would be) too complicated for any human mind to hold it all together or even to keep on attending. But that, again, would be a defect in the human instrument, not in Reason. A sum in simple arithmetic may be too long and complicated for a child's limited powers of concentration: but it is not a radically different kind of thing from the short sums the child *can* do.

Now it seems to me that the relation between our sense of values and the values acknowledged by the cosmic or super-cosmic Reason is likely to be the same as the relation between our attempts at logic and Logic itself. It is, I admit, conceivable that the ultimate Reason acknowledges no values at all: but that theory, as I have tried to show, is inconsistent with our continuing to attach any importance to our own values. And since everyone in fact intends to continue doing so, that theory is not really a live option. But if we attribute a sense of value to the ultimate Reason, I do not think we can suppose it to be totally different from our own sense of value. If it were, then our own sense of value would have to be merely human: and from that all the same consequences would flow as from an admission that the supreme mind acknowledged no values at all. Indeed to say that a mind has a sense of values *totally* different from the only values we can conceive is to say that that mind has we know not what: which is precious near saying nothing particular about it. It would also be very odd, on the supposition that our sense of values is a mere illusion, that education, rationality, and enlightenment show no tendency to remove it from human minds. And at this stage in the argument there is really no inducement to do any of these rather desperate things. The *prima facie* case for denying a sense of values to the cosmic or super-cosmic mind has really collapsed the moment we see that we have to attribute reason to it. When we are forced to admit that reason cannot be merely human, there is no longer any compulsive inducement to say that virtue is purely human. If wisdom turns out to be something objective and external, it is at least probable that goodness will turn out to be the same. But here also it is reasonable to combine a firm belief in the objective validity of goodness with a considerable scepticism about all our particular moral judgements. To say that they all require correction is indeed to say both that they are partially wrong and that they are not merely subjective facts about ourselves—for if that were so the process of enlightenment would consist not in correcting them but in abandoning them altogether.

There is, to be sure, one glaringly obvious ground for denying that any moral purpose at all is operative in the universe: namely, the actual course of events in all its wasteful cruelty and apparent indifference, or hostility, to life. But then, as I maintain, that is precisely the ground which we cannot use. Unless we judge this waste and cruelty to be real evils we cannot of course condemn the universe for exhibiting them. Unless we take our own standard of goodness to be valid in principle (however fallible our particular applications of it) we cannot mean anything by calling waste and cruelty evils. And unless we take our own standard to be something more than ours, to be in fact an objective principle to which we are responding, we cannot regard that standard as valid. In a word, unless we allow ultimate reality to be moral, we cannot morally condemn it. The more seriously we take our own charge of futility the more we are committed to the implication that reality in the last resort is not futile at all. The defiance of the good atheist hurled at an apparently ruthless and idiotic cosmos is really an unconscious homage to something in or behind that cosmos which he recognizes as infinitely valuable and authoritative: for if mercy and justice were really only private whims of his own with no objective and impersonal roots, and if he realized this, he could not go on being indignant. The fact that he arraigns heaven itself for disregarding them means that at some level of his mind he knows they are enthroned in a higher heaven still.

I cannot and never could persuade myself that such defiance is displeasing to the supreme mind. There is something holier about the atheism of a Shelley than about the theism of a Paley. That is the lesson of the Book of Job. No explanation of the problem of unjust suffering is there given: that is not the point of the poem. The point is that the man who accepts our ordinary standard of good and by it hotly criticizes divine justice receives the divine approval: the orthodox, pious people who palter with that standard in the attempt to justify God are condemned. Apparently the way to advance from our imperfect apprehension of justice to the absolute justice is *not* to throw our imperfect apprehensions aside but boldly to go on applying them. Just as the pupil advances to more perfect arithmetic not by throwing his multiplication table away but by working it for all it is worth.

Of course no one will be content to leave the matter just where the Book of Job leaves it. But that is as far as I intend to go tonight. Having grasped the truth that our very condemnation of reality carries in its heart an unconscious act of allegiance to that same reality as the source of our moral standards, we then of course have to ask how this ultimate morality in the universe can be reconciled with the actual course of events. It is really the same sort of problem that meets us in science. The pell-mell of phenomena, as we first observe them, seems to be full of anomalies and irregularities; but being assured that reality is logical we go on framing and trying out hypotheses to show that the apparent irregularities are not really irregular at all. The history of science is the history of that process. The corresponding process whereby, having admitted that reality in the last resort must be moral, we attempt to explain evil, is the history of theology. Into that theological inquiry I do not propose to go at present. If any of you thinks of pursuing it, I would risk giving him one piece of advice. I think he can save himself time by confining his attention to two systems—Hinduism and Christianity. I believe these are the two serious options for an adult mind. Materialism is a philosophy for boys. The purely moral systems like Stoicism and Confucianism are philosophies for aristocrats. Islam is only a Christian heresy, and Buddhism a Hindu heresy: both are simplifications inferior to the things simplified. As for the old Pagan religions, I think we could say that whatever was of value in them survives either in Hinduism or in Christianity or in both, and there only: they are the two systems which have come down, still alive, into the present without leaving the past behind them.

But all that is a matter for further consideration. I aim tonight only at reversing the popular belief that reality is totally alien to our minds. My answer to that view consists simply in restating it in the form: 'Our minds are totally alien to reality.' Put that way, it reveals itself as a self-contradiction. For if our minds are totally alien to reality then all our thoughts, including this thought, are worthless. We must, then, grant logic to the reality; we must, if we are to have any moral standards, grant it moral standards too. And there is really no reason why we should not do the same about standards of beauty. There is no reason why our reaction to a beautiful landscape should not be the response, however humanly blurred and partial, to a something that is really there. The idea of a wholly mindless and valueless universe has to be abandoned at one point—i.e. as regards logic: after that, there is no telling at how many other points it will be defeated nor how great the reversal of our nineteenth century philosophy must finally be.

THE POISON OF SUBJECTIVISM

One cause of misery and vice is always present with us in the greed and pride of men, but at certain periods in history this is greatly increased by the temporary prevalence of some false philosophy. Correct thinking will not make good men of bad ones; but a purely theoretical error may remove ordinary checks to evil and deprive good intentions of their natural support. An error of this sort is abroad at present. I am not referring to the Power philosophies of the Totalitarian states, but to something that goes deeper and spreads wider and which, indeed, has given these Power philosophies their golden opportunity. I am referring to Subjectivism.

After studying his environment man has begun to study himself. Up to that point, he had assumed his own reason and through it seen all other things. Now, his own reason has become the object: it is as if we took out our eyes to look at them. Thus studied, his own reason appears to him as the epiphenomenon which accompanies chemical or electrical events in a cortex which is itself the by-product of a blind evolutionary process. His own logic, hitherto the king whom events in all possible worlds must obey, becomes merely subjective. There is no reason for supposing that it yields truth.

As long as this dethronement refers only to the theoretical reason, it cannot be wholehearted. The scientist has to assume the validity of his own logic (in the stout old fashion of Plato or Spinoza) even in order to prove that it is merely subjective, and therefore he can only flirt with subjectivism. It is true that this flirtation sometimes goes pretty far. There are modern scientists, I am told, who have dropped the words *truth* and *reality* out of their vocabulary and who hold that the end of their work is not to know what is there but simply to get practical results. This is, no doubt, a bad symptom. But, in the main, subjectivism is such an uncomfortable yokefellow for research that the danger, in this quarter, is continually counteracted.

But when we turn to practical reason the ruinous effects are

72

found operating in full force. By practical reason I mean our judgement of good and evil. If you are surprised that I include this under the heading of reason at all, let me remind you that your surprise is itself one result of the subjectivism I am discussing. Until modern times no thinker of the first rank ever doubted that our judgements of value were rational judgements or that what they discovered was objective. It was taken for granted that in temptation passion was opposed, not to some sentiment, but to reason. Thus Plato thought, thus Aristotle, thus Hooker, Butler and Doctor Johnson. The modern view is very different. It does not believe that value judgements are really judgements at all. They are sentiments, or complexes, or attitudes, produced in a community by the pressure of its environment and its traditions, and differing from one community to another. To say that a thing is good is merely to express our feeling about it; and our feeling about it is the feeling we have been socially conditioned to have.

But if this is so, then we might have been conditioned to feel otherwise. 'Perhaps', thinks the reformer or the educational expert, 'it would be better if we were. Let us improve our morality.' Out of this apparently innocent idea comes the disease that will certainly end our species (and, in my view, damn our souls) if it is not crushed; the fatal superstition that men can create values, that a community can choose its 'ideology' as men choose their clothes. Everyone is indignant when he hears the Germans define justice as that which is to the interest of the Third Reich. But it is not always remembered that this indignation is perfectly groundless if we ourselves regard morality as a subjective sentiment to be altered at will. Unless there is some objective standard of good, over-arching Germans, Japanese and ourselves alike whether any of us obey it or no, then of course the Germans are as competent to create their ideology as we are to create ours. If 'good' and 'better' are terms deriving their sole meaning from the ideology of each people, then of course ideologies themselves cannot be better or worse than one another. Unless the measuring rod is independent of the things measured, we can do no measuring. For the same reason it is useless to compare the moral ideas of one age with those of another: progress and decadence are alike meaningless words.

All this is so obvious that it amounts to an identical proposition. But how little it is now understood can be gauged from the procedure of the moral reformer who, after saying that 'good' means 'what we are conditioned to like' goes on cheerfully to consider whether it might be 'better' that we should be conditioned to like something else. What in Heaven's names does he mean by 'better'?

He usually has at the back of his mind the notion that if he throws over traditional judgement of value, he will find something else, something more 'real' or 'solid' on which to base a new scheme of values. He will say, for example, 'We must abandon irrational taboos and base our values on the good of the community'—as if the maxim 'Thou shalt promote the good of the community' were anything more than a polysyllabic variant of 'Do as you would be done by' which has itself no other basis than the old universal value judgement he claims to be rejecting. Or he will endeavour to base his values on biology and tell us that we must act thus and thus for the preservation of our species. Apparently he does not anticipate the question, 'Why should the species be preserved?' He takes it for granted that it should, because he is really relying on traditional judgements of value. If he were starting, as he pretends, with a clean slate, he could never reach this principle. Sometimes he tries to do so by falling back on 'instinct'. 'We have an instinct to preserve our species', he may say. But have we? And if we have, who told us that we must obey our instincts? And why should we obey this instinct in the teeth of many others which conflict with the preservation of the species? The reformer knows that some instincts are to be obeyed more than others only because he is judging instincts by a standard, and the standard is, once more, the traditional morality which he claims to be superseding. The instincts themselves obviously cannot furnish us with grounds for grading the instincts in a hierarchy. If you do not bring a knowledge of their comparative respectability *to* your study of them, you can never derive it *from* them.

This whole attempt to jettison traditional values as something subjective and to substitute a new scheme of values for them is wrong. It is like trying to lift yourself by your own coat collar. Let us get two propositions written into our minds with indelible ink.

(1) The human mind has no more power of inventing a new value than of planting a new sun in the sky or a new primary colour in the spectrum.

(2) Every attempt to do so consists in arbitrarily selecting some one maxim of traditional morality, isolating it from the rest, and erecting it into an *unum necessarium*.

The second proposition will bear a little illustration. Ordinary morality tells us to honour our parents and cherish our children. By taking the second precept alone you construct a Futurist Ethic in which the claims of 'posterity' are the sole criterion. Ordinary morality tells us to keep promises and also to feed the hungry. By taking the second precept alone you get a Communist Ethic in which 'production', and distribution of the products to the people, are the sole criteria. Ordinary morality tells us, *ceteris paribus*, to love our kindred and fellow-citizens more than strangers. By isolating this precept you can get either an Aristocratic Ethic with the claims of our class as sole criterion, or a Racialist Ethic where no claims but those of blood are acknowledged. These monomaniac systems are then used as a ground from which to attack traditional morality; but absurdly, since it is from traditional morality alone that they derive such semblance of validity as they possess. Starting from scratch, with no assumptions about value, we could reach none of them. If reverence for parents or promises is a mere subjective by-product of physical nature, so is reverence for race or posterity. The trunk to whose root the reformer would lay the axe is the only support of the particular branch he wishes to retain.

All idea of 'new' or 'scientific' or 'modern' moralities must therefore be dismissed as mere confusion of thought. We have only two alternatives. Either the maxims of traditional morality must be accepted as axioms of practical reason which neither admit nor require argument to support them and not to 'see' which is to have lost human status; or else there are no values at all, what we mistook for values being 'projections' of irrational emotions. It is perfectly futile, after having dismissed traditional morality with the question, 'Why should we obey it?' then to attempt the reintroduction of value at some later stage in our philosophy. Any value we reintroduce can be countered in just the same way. Every argument used to support it will be an attempt to derive from premises in the indicative mood a conclusion in the imperative. And this is impossible.

Against this view the modern mind has two lines of defence. The first claims that traditional morality is different in different times and places—in fact, that there is not one morality but a thousand. The second exclaims that to tie ourselves to an immutable moral code is to cut off all progress and acquiesce in 'stagnation'. Both are unsound.

Let us take the second one first. And let us strip it of the illegitimate emotional power it derives from the word 'stagnation' with its suggestion of puddles and mantled pools. If water stands too long it stinks. To infer thence that whatever stands long must be unwholesome is to be the victim of metaphor. Space does not stink because it has preserved its three dimensions from the beginning. The square on the hypotenuse has not gone mouldy by continuing to equal the sum of the squares on the other two sides. Love is not dishonoured by constancy, and when we wash our hands we are seeking stagnation and 'putting the clock back', artificially restoring our hands to the *status quo* in which they began the day and resisting the natural trend of events which would increase their dirtiness steadily from our birth to our death. For the emotive term 'stagnant' let us substitute the descriptive term 'permanent'. Does a permanent moral standard preclude progress? On the contrary, except on the supposition of a changeless standard, progress is impossible. If good is a fixed point, it is at least possible that we should get nearer and nearer to it; but if the terminus is as mobile as the train, how can the train progress towards it? Our ideas of the good may change, but they cannot change either for the better or the worse if there is no absolute and immutable good to which they can approximate or from which they can recede. We can go on getting a sum more and more nearly right only if the one perfectly right answer is 'stagnant'.

And yet it will be said, I have just admitted that our ideas of good may improve. How is this to be reconciled with the view that 'traditional morality' is a *depositum fidei* which cannot be deserted? The answer can be understood if we compare a real moral advance with a mere innovation. From the Stoic and Confucian, 'Do not do to others what you would not like them to do to you'; to the Christian, 'Do as you would be done by' is a real advance. The morality of Nietzsche is a mere innovation. The first is an advance because no one who did not admit the validity of the old maxim could see reason for accepting the new one, and anyone who accepted the old would at once recognize the new as an extension of the same principle. If he rejected it, he would have to reject it as a superfluity, something that went too far, not as something simply heterogeneous from his own ideas of value. But the Nietzschean ethic can be accepted only if we are ready to scrap traditional morals as a mere error and then to put ourselves in a position where we can find no ground for any value judgements at all. It is the difference between a man who says to us: 'You like your vegetables moderately fresh; why not grow your own and have them perfectly fresh?' and a man who says, 'Throw away that loaf and try eating bricks and centipedes instead.' Real moral advances, in fine, are made *from within* the existing moral tradition and in the spirit of that tradition and can be understood only in the light of that tradition. The outsider who has rejected the tradition cannot judge them. He has, as Aristotle said, no *arche*, no premises.

And what of the second modern objection—that the ethical standards of different cultures differ so widely that there is no common tradition at all? The answer is that this is a lie—a good, solid, resounding lie. If a man will go into a library and spend a few days with the *Encyclopedia of Religion and Ethics* he will soon discover the massive unanimity of the practical reason in man. From the Babylonian *Hymn to Samos*, from the Laws of Manu, the *Book of the Dead*, the Analects, the Stoics, the Platonists, from Australian aborigines and Redskins, he will collect the same triumphantly monotonous denunciations of oppression, murder, treachery and falsehood, the same injunctions of kindness to the aged, the young, and the weak, of almsgiving and impartiality and honesty. He may be a little surprised (I certainly was) to find that precepts of mercy are more frequent than precepts of justice; but he will no longer doubt that there is such a thing as the Law of Nature. There are, of course, differences. There are even blindnesses in particular cultures—just as there are savages who cannot count up to twenty. But the pretence that we are presented with a mere chaos—though no outline of universally accepted value shows through—is simply false and should be contradicted in season and out of season wherever it is met. Far from finding a chaos, we find exactly what we should expect if good is indeed something objective and reason the organ whereby it is apprehended—that is, a substantial agreement with considerable local differences of emphasis and, perhaps, no one code that includes everything.

The two grand methods of obscuring this agreement are these: First, you can concentrate on those divergences about sexual morality which most serious moralists regard as belonging to positive rather than to Natural Law, but which rouse strong emotions. Differences about the definition of incest or between polygamy and monogamy come under this head. (It is untrue to say that the Greeks thought sexual perversion innocent. The continual tittering of Plato is really more evidential than the stern prohibition of Aristotle. Men titter thus only about what they regard as, at least, a *peccadillo*: the jokes about drunkenness in *Pickwick*, far from proving that the nineteenth-century English thought it innocent, prove the reverse. There is an enormous difference of *degree* between the Greek view of perversion and the Christian, but there is not opposition.) The second method is to treat as differences in the judgement of value what are really differences in belief about fact. Thus human sacrifice, or persecution of witches, are cited as evidence of a radically different morality. But the real difference lies elsewhere. We do not hunt witches because we disbelieve in their existence. We do not kill men to avert pestilence because we do not think pestilence can thus be averted. We do 'sacrifice' men in war, and we do hunt spies and traitors.

So far I have been considering the objections which unbelievers bring against the doctrine of objective value, or the Law of Nature. But in our days we must be prepared to meet objections from Christians too. 'Humanism' and 'liberalism' are coming to be used simply as terms of disapprobation, and both are likely to be so used of the position I am taking up. Behind them lurks a real theological problem. If we accept the primary platitudes of practical reason as the unquestioned premises of all action, are we thereby trusting our own reason so far that we ignore the Fall, and are we retrogressively turning our absolute allegiance away from a person to an abstraction?

As regards the Fall, I submit that the general tenor of scripture does not encourage us to believe that our knowledge of the Law has been depraved in the same degree as our power to fulfil it. He would be a brave man who claimed to realize the fallen condition of man more clearly than St Paul. In that very chapter (Romans 7) where he asserts most strongly our inability to keep the moral law he also asserts most confidently that we perceive the Law's goodness and rejoice in it according to the inward man. Our righteousness may be filthy and ragged; but Christianity gives us no ground for holding that our perceptions of right are in the same condition. They may, no doubt, be impaired; but there is a difference between imperfect sight and blindness. A theology which goes about to represent our practical reason as radically unsound is heading for disaster. If we once admit that what God means by 'goodness' is sheerly different from what we judge to be good, there is no difference left between pure religion and devil worship.

The other objection is much more formidable. If we once grant that our practical reason is really reason and that its fundamental imperatives are as absolute and categorical as they claim to be, then unconditional allegiance to them is the duty of man. So is absolute allegiance to God. And these two allegiances must, somehow, be the same. But how is the relation between God and the moral law to be represented? To say that the moral law is God's law is no final solution. Are these things right because God commands them or does God command them because they are right? If the first, if good is to be *defined* as what God commands, then the goodness of God Himself is emptied of meaning and the commands of an omnipotent fiend would have the same claim on us as those of the 'righteous Lord'. If the second, then we seem to be admitting a cosmic dyarchy, or even making God Himself the mere executor of a law somehow external and antecedent to His own being. Both views are intolerable.

At this point we must remind ourselves that Christian theology does not believe God to be a person. It believes Him to be such that in Him a trinity of persons is consistent with a unity of Deity. In that sense it believes Him to be something very different from a person, just as a cube, in which six squares are consistent with unity of the body, is different from a square. (Flatlanders, attempting to imagine a cube, would either imagine the six squares coinciding, and thus destroy their distinctness, or else imagine them set out side by side, and thus destroy the unity. Our difficulties about the Trinity are much of the same kind.) It is therefore possible that the duality which seems to force itself upon us when we think, first, of our Father in Heaven, and, secondly, of the self-evident imperatives of the moral law, is not a mere error but a real (though inadequate and creaturely) perception of things that would necessarily be two in any mode of being which enters our experience, but which are not so divided in the absolute being of the superpersonal God. When we attempt to think of a person and a law, we are compelled to think of this person either as obeying the law or as making it. And when we think of Him as making it we are compelled to think of Him either as making it in conformity to some yet more ultimate pattern of goodness (in which case that pattern, and not He, would be supreme) or else as making it arbitrarily by a *sic volo, sic jubeo* (in which case He would be neither good nor wise). But it is probably just here that our categories betray us. It would be idle, with our merely mortal resources, to attempt a positive correction of our categories—*ambularvi in mirabilibus supra me.* But it might be permissible to lay down two negations: that God neither *obeys* nor *creates* the moral law. The good is uncreated; it never could have been otherwise; it has in it no shadow of contingency; it lies, as Plato said, on the other side of existence. It is the *Rita* of the Hindus by which the gods themselves are divine, the *Tao* of the Chinese from which all realities proceed. But we, favoured beyond the wisest pagans, know what lies beyond existence, what admits no contingency, what lends divinity to all else, what is the ground of all existence, is not simply a law but also a begetting love, a love begotten, and the love which, being between these two, is also imminent in all those who are caught up to share the unity of their self-caused life. God is not merely good, but goodness; goodness is not merely divine, but God.

These may seem fine-spun speculations: yet I believe that nothing short of this can save us. A Christianity which does not see moral and religious experience converging to meet at infinity, not at a negative infinity, but in the positive infinity of the living yet superpersonal God, has nothing, in the long run, to divide it from devil worship; and a philosophy which does not accept value as eternal and objective can lead us only to ruin. Nor is the matter of merely speculative importance. Many a popular 'planner' on a democratic platform, many a mild-eyed scientist in a democratic laboratory means, in the last resort, just what the Fascist means. He believes that 'good' means whatever men are conditioned to approve. He believes that it is the function of him and his kind to condition men; to create consciences by eugenics, psychological manipulation of infants, state education and mass propaganda. Because he is confused, he does not yet fully realize that those who create conscience cannot be subject to conscience themselves. But he must awake to the logic of his position sooner or later; and when he does, what barrier remains between us and the final division of the race into a few condition-ers who stand themselves outside morality and the many con-ditioned in whom such morality as the experts choose is produced at the experts' pleasure? If 'good' means only the local ideology, how can those who invent the local ideology be guided by any idea of good themselves? The very idea of freedom presupposes some objective moral law which overarches rulers and ruled alike. Subjectivism about values is eternally incompatible with democracy. We and our rulers are of one kind only so long as we are subject to one law. But if there is no Law of Nature, the *ethos* of any society is the creation of its rulers, educators and con-ditioners; and every creator stands above and outside his own creation.

Unless we return to the crude and nursery-like belief in ob-jective values, we perish. If we do, we may live, and such a return might have one minor advantage. If we believed in the absolute reality of elementary moral platitudes, we should value those who solicit our votes by other standards than have recently been in fashion. While we believe that good is something to be invented, we demand of our rulers such qualities as 'vision', 'dynamism', 'creativity', and the like. If we returned to the objective view we should demand qualities much rarer, and much more beneficial—virtue, knowledge, diligence and skill. 'Vision' is for sale, or claims to be for sale, everywhere. But give me a man who will do a day's work for a day's pay, who will refuse bribes, who will not make up his facts, and who has learned his job.

THE FUNERAL OF A GREAT MYTH

There are some mistakes which humanity has made and repented so often that there is now really no excuse for making them again. One of these is the injustice which every age does to its predecessor; for example, the ignorant contempt which the Humanists (even good Humanists like Sir Thomas More) felt for medieval philosophy or Romantics (even good Romantics like Keats) felt for eighteenth-century poetry. Each time all this 'reaction' and resentment has to be punished and unsaid; it is a wasteful performance. It is tempting to try whether we, at least, cannot avoid it. Why should we not give our predecessors a fair and filial dismissal?

Such, at all events, is the attempt I am going to make in this paper. I come to bury the great Myth of the nineteenth and early twentieth Century; but also to praise it. I am going to pronounce a funeral oration.

By this great Myth I mean that picture of reality which resulted during the period under consideration, not logically but imaginatively, from some of the more striking and (so to speak) marketable theories of the real scientists. I have heard this Myth called 'Wellsianity'. The name is a good one in so far as it does justice to the share which a great imaginative writer bore in building it up. But it is not satisfactory. It suggests, as we shall see, an error about the date at which the Myth became dominant; and it also suggests that the Myth affected only the 'middle-brow' mind. In fact it is as much behind Bridges' *Testament of Beauty* as it is behind the work of Wells. It dominates minds as different as those of Professor Alexander and Walt Disney. It is implicit in nearly every modern article on politics, sociology, and ethics.

I call it a Myth because it is, as I have said, the imaginative and not the logical result of what is vaguely called 'modern science'. Strictly speaking, there is, I confess, no such thing as 'modern science'. There are only particular sciences, all in a stage of rapid change, and sometimes inconsistent with one another. What the Myth uses is a selection from the scientific theories—a selection made at first, and modified afterwards, in obedience to imaginative and emotional needs. It is the work of the folk imagination, moved by its natural appetite for an impressive unity. It therefore treats its *data* with great freedom—selecting, slurring, expurgating, and adding at will.

The central idea of the Myth is what its believers would call 'Evolution' or 'Development' or 'Emergence', just as the central idea in the myth of Adonis is Death and Re-birth. I do not mean that the doctrine of Evolution as held by practising biologists is a Myth. It may be shown, by later biologists, to be a less satisfactory hypothesis than was hoped fifty years ago. But that does not amount to being a Myth. It is a genuine scientific hypothesis. But we must sharply distinguish between Evolution as a biological theorem and popular Evolutionism or Developmentalism which is certainly a Myth. Before proceeding to describe it and (which is my chief business) to pronounce its eulogy, I had better make clear its mythical character.

We have, first of all, the evidence of chronology. If popular Evolutionism were (as it imagines itself to be) not a Myth but the intellectually legitimate result of the scientific theorem on the public mind, it would arise *after* that theorem had become widely known. We should have the theorem known first of all to a few, then adopted by all the scientists, then spreading to all men of general education, then beginning to affect poetry and the arts, and so finally percolating to the mass of the people. In fact, however, we find something quite different. The clearest and finest poetical expressions of the Myth come before the *Origin of Species* was published (1859) and long before it had established itself as scientific orthodoxy. There had, to be sure, been hints and germs of the theory in scientific circles before 1859. But if the mythopoeic poets were at all infected by those germs they must have been very up-to-date indeed, very predisposed to catch the infection. Almost before the scientists spoke, certainly before they spoke clearly, imagination was ripe for it.

The finest expression of the Myth in English does not come from Bridges, nor from Shaw, nor from Wells, nor from Olaf Stapledon. It is this:

As Heaven and Earth are fairer, fairer far
Than Chaos and blank Darkness, though once chief;
And as we show beyond that Heaven and Earth
In form and shape compact and beautiful,
In will, in action free, companionship,
And thousand other signs of purer life;
So on our heels a fresh perfection treads,
A power more strong in beauty, born of us,
And fated to excel us, as we pass
In glory that old Darkness.

Thus Oceanus, in Keats's *Hyperion*, nearly forty years before the *Origin of the Species*. And on the continent we have the *Nibelung's Ring*. Coming, as I do, to bury but also to praise the receding age, I will by no means join in the modern depreciation of Wagner. He may, for all I know, have been a bad man. He may (though I shall never believe it) have been a bad musician. But as a mythopoeic poet he is incomparable. The tragedy of the Evolutionary Myth has never been more nobly expressed than in his Wotan: its heady raptures never more irresistibly than in *Siegfried*. That he himself knew quite well what he was writing about can be seen from his letter to August Rockel in 1854. 'The progress of the whole drama shows the necessity of recognizing and submitting to the change, the diversity, the multiplicity, the eternal novelty, of the Real. Wotan rises to the tragic height of willing his own downfall. This is all we have to learn from the history of Man—to will the necessary and ourselves to bring it to pass.'

If Shaw's *Back to Methuselah* were really, as he supposed, the work of a prophet or a pioneer ushering in the reign of a new Myth, its predominantly comic tone and its generally low emotional temperature would be inexplicable. It is admirable fun: but not thus are new epochs brought to birth. The ease with which he plays with the Myth shows that the Myth is fully digested and already senile. Shaw is the Lucian or the Snorri of this mythology: to find its Aeschylus or its Elder Edda you must go back to Keats and Wagner.

That, then, is the first proof that popular Evolution is a Myth. In making it Imagination runs ahead of scientific evidence. 'The prophetic soul of the big world' was already pregnant with the

Myth: if science has not met the imaginative need, science would not have been so popular. But probably every age gets, within certain limits, the science it desires.

In the second place we have internal evidence. Popular Evolutionism or Developmentalism differs *in content* from the Evolution of the real biologists. To the biologist Evolution is a hypothesis. It covers more of the facts than any other hypothesis at present on the market and is therefore to be accepted unless, or until, some new supposal can be shown to cover still more facts with even fewer assumptions. At least, that is what I think most biologists would say. Professor D. M. S. Watson, it is true, would not go so far. According to him Evolution 'is accepted by zoologists not because it has been observed to occur or . . . can be proved by logically coherent evidence to be true, but because the only alternative, special creation, is clearly incredible'. (Watson, quoted in *Nineteenth Century* (April 1943), 'Science and the B.B.C.') This would mean that the sole ground for believing it is not empirical but metaphysical—the dogma of an amateur metaphysician who finds 'special creation' incredible. But I do not think it has really come to that. Most biologists have a more robust belief in Evolution than Professor Watson. But it is certainly a hypothesis. In the Myth, however, there is nothing hypothetical about it: it is basic fact: or, to speak more strictly, such distinctions do not exist on the mythical level at all. There are more important differences to follow.

In the science, Evolution is a theory about *changes*: in the Myth it is a fact about *improvements*. Thus a real scientist like Professor J. B. S. Haldane is at pains to point out that popular ideas of Evolution lay a wholly unjustified emphasis on those changes which have rendered creatures (by human standards) 'better' or more interesting. He adds: 'We are therefore inclined to regard progress as the rule in evolution. Actually it is the exception, and for every case of it there are ten of degeneration.'[1] But the Myth simply expurgates the ten cases of degeneration. In the popular mind the word 'Evolution' conjures up a picture of things moving 'onwards and upwards', and of nothing else whatsoever. And it might have been predicted that it would do so. Already, before science had spoken, the mythical imagination knew the kind of

[1] 'Darwinism Today', *Possible Worlds*, p. 28.

'Evolution' it wanted. It wanted the Keatian and Wagnerian kind: the gods superseding the Titans, and the young, joyous, careless, amorous Siegfried superseding the care-worn, anxious, treaty-entangled Wotan. If science offers any instances to satisfy that demand, they will be eagerly accepted. If it offers any instances that frustrate it, they will simply be ignored.

Again, for the scientist Evolution is a purely biological theorem. It takes over organic life on this planet as a going concern and tries to explain certain changes within that field. It makes no cosmic statements, no metaphysical statements, no eschatological statements. Granted that we now have minds we can trust, granted that organic life came to exist, it tries to explain, say, how a species that once had wings came to lose them. It explains this by the negative effect of environment operating on small variations. It does not in itself explain the origin of organic life, nor of the variations, nor does it discuss the origin and validity of reason. It may well tell you how the brain, through which reason now operates, arose, but that is a different matter. Still less does it even attempt to tell you how the universe as a whole arose, or what it is, or whither it is tending. But the Myth knows none of these reticences. Having first turned what was a theory of change into a theory of improvement, it then makes this a *cosmic* theory. Not merely terrestrial organisms but *everything* is moving 'upwards and onwards'. Reason has 'evolved' out of instinct, virtue out of complexes, poetry out of erotic howls and grunts, civilization out of savagery, the organic out of inorganic, the solar system out of some sidereal soup or traffic block. And conversely, reason, virtue, art and civilization as we now know them are only the crude or embryonic beginnings of far better things—perhaps Deity itself—in the remote future. For in the Myth, 'Evolution' (as the Myth understands it) is the formula of *all* existence. To exist means to be moving from the status of 'almost zero' to the status of 'almost infinity'. To those brought up on the Myth nothing seems more normal, more natural, more plausible, than that chaos should turn into order, death into life, ignorance into knowledge. And with this we reach the full-blown Myth. It is one of the most moving and satisfying world dramas which have ever been imagined.

The drama proper is preceded (do not forget the Rheingold

here) by the most austere of all preludes; the infinite void and matter endlessly, aimlessly moving to bring forth it knows not what. Then by some millionth, millionth chance—what tragic irony!—the conditions at one point of space and time bubble up into that tiny fermentation which we call organic life. At first everything seems to be against the infant hero of our drama; just as everything always was against the seventh son or ill-used step-daughter in a fairy tale. But life somehow wins through. With incalculable sufferings (the Sorrows of the Volsungs were nothing to it), against all but insuperable obstacles, it spreads, it breeds, it complicates itself; from the amoeba up to the reptile, up to the mammal. Life (here comes our first climax) 'wantons as in her prime'. This is the age of monsters: dragons prowl the earth, devour one another, and die. Then the old irresistible theme of the Younger Son or the Ugly Duckling is repeated. As the weak, tiny spark of life herself began amidst the beasts that are far larger and stronger than he, there comes forth a little, naked, shivering, cowering biped, shuffling, not yet fully erect, promising nothing: the product of another millionth, millionth chance. His name in this Myth is Man: elsewhere he has been the young Beowulf whom men at first thought a dastard, or the stripling David armed only with a sling against mail-clad Goliath, or Jack the Giant-Killer himself, or even Hop-o'-my-Thumb. He thrives. He begins killing his giants. He becomes the Cave Man with his flints and his club, muttering and growling over his enemies' bones, almost a brute yet somehow able to invent art, pottery, language, weapons, cookery and nearly everything else (his name in another story is Robinson Crusoe), dragging his screaming mate by her hair (I do not exactly know why), tearing his children to pieces in fierce jealousy until they are old enough to tear him, and cowering before the terrible gods whom he has invented in his own image.

But these were only growing pains. In the next act he has become true Man. He learns to master Nature. Science arises and dissipates the superstitions of his infancy. More and more he becomes the controller of his own fate. Passing hastily over the historical period (in it the upward and onward movement gets in places a little indistinct, but it is a mere nothing by the time-scale we are using) we follow our hero on into the future. See him in the last act, though not the last scene, of this great mystery. A race of demi-gods now rule the planet (in some versions, the galaxy). Eugenics have made certain that only demi-gods will now be born: psycho-analysis that none of them shall lose or smirch his divinity: economics that they shall have to hand all that demi-gods require. Man has ascended his throne. Man has become God. All is a blaze of glory. And now, mark well the final stroke of mythopoeic genius. It is only the more debased versions of the Myth that end here. For to end here is a little bathetic, even a little vulgar. If we stopped at this point the story would lack the highest grandeur. Therefore, in the best versions, the last scene reverses all. Arthur died: Siegfried died: Roland died at Roncesvaux. Dusk steals darkly over the gods. All this time we have forgotten Mordred, Hagen, Ganilon. All this time Nature, the old enemy who only seemed to be defeated, has been gnawing away, silently, unceasingly, out of the reach of human power. The Sun will cool —all suns will cool—the whole universe will run down. Life (every form of life) will be banished without hope of return from every cubic inch of infinite space. All ends in nothingness. 'Universal darkness covers all.' True to the shape of Elizabethan tragedy, the hero has swiftly fallen from the glory to which he slowly climbed: we are dismissed 'in the calm of mind, all passion spent'. It is indeed much better than an Elizabethan tragedy, for it has a more complete finality. It brings us to the end not of a story, but of all possible stories: *enden sah ich die welt.*

I grew up believing in this Myth and I have felt—I still feel—its almost perfect grandeur. Let no one say we are an unimaginative age: neither the Greeks nor the Norsemen ever invented a better story. Even to the present day, in certain moods, I could almost find it in my heart to wish that it was not mythical, but true.[1] And yet, how could it be?

What makes it impossible that it should be true is not so much the lack of evidence for this or that scene in the drama or the fatal self-contradiction which runs right through it. The Myth

[1 In a paper read to the Oxford Socratic Club on 'Is Theology Poetry?', Lewis admits that if Christian Theology were only a myth he would not find even it as attractive as the Myth considered in this paper: 'Christianity offers the attraction neither of optimism nor of pessimism. It represents the life of the universe as being very like the mortal life of men on this planet—"of a mingled yarn, good and ill together."' *The Socratic Digest* (1945).]

cannot even get going without accepting a good deal from the real sciences. And the real sciences cannot be accepted for a moment unless rational inferences are valid: for every science claims to be a series of inferences from observed facts. It is only by such inferences that you can reach your nebulae and protoplasm and dinosaurs and sub-men and cave-men at all. Unless you start by believing that reality in the remotest space and the remotest time rigidly obeys the laws of logic, you can have no ground for believing in any astronomy, any biology, any palaeontology, any archaeology. To reach the positions held by the real scientists—which are then taken over by the Myth—you must—in fact, treat reason as an absolute. But at the same time the Myth asks me to believe that reason is simply the unforeseen and unintended by-product of a mindless process at one stage of its endless and aimless becoming. The content of the Myth thus knocks from under me the only ground on which I could possibly believe the Myth to be true. If my own mind is a product of the irrational—if what seem my clearest reasonings are only the way in which a creature conditioned as I am is bound to feel—how shall I trust my mind when it tells me about Evolution? They say in effect 'I will prove that what you call a proof is only the result of mental habits which result from heredity which results from bio-chemistry which results from physics.' But this is the same as saying: 'I will prove that proofs are irrational': more succinctly, 'I will prove that there are no proofs': The fact that some people of scientific education cannot by any effort be taught to see the difficulty, confirms one's suspicion that we here touch a radical disease in their whole style of thought. But the man who does see it, is compelled to reject as mythical the cosmology in which most of us were brought up. That it has embedded in it many true particulars I do not doubt: but in its entirety, it simply will not do. Whatever the real universe may turn out to be like, it can't be like that.

I have been speaking hitherto of this Myth as of a thing to be buried because I believe that its dominance is already over; in the sense that what seem to me to be the most vigorous movements of contemporary thought point away from it. Physics (a discipline less easily mythological) is replacing biology as the science *par excellence* in the mind of the plain man. The whole philosophy of Becoming has been vigorously challenged by the American

'Humanists'. The revival of theology has attained proportions that have to be reckoned with. The Romantic poetry and music in which popular Evolutionism found their natural counterpart are going out of fashion. But of course a Myth does not die in a day. We may expect that this Myth, when driven from cultured circles, will long retain its hold on the masses, and even when abandoned by them will continue for centuries to haunt our language. Those who wish to attack it must beware of despising it. There are deep reasons for its popularity.

The basic idea of the Myth—that small or chaotic or feeble things perpetually turn themselves into large, strong, ordered things—may, at first sight, seem a very odd one. We have never actually seen a pile of rubble turning itself into a house. But this odd idea commends itself to the imagination by the help of what seem to be two instances of it within everyone's knowledge. Everyone has seen individual organisms doing it. Acorns become oaks, grubs become insects, eggs become birds, every man was once an embryo. And secondly—which weighs very much in the popular mind during a machine age—everyone has seen Evolution really happening in the history of machines. We all remember when locomotives were smaller and less efficient than they are now. These two apparent instances are quite enough to convince the imagination that Evolution in a cosmic sense is the most natural thing in the world. It is true that reason cannot here agree with imagination. These apparent instances are not really instances of Evolution at all. The oak comes indeed from the acorn, but then the acorn was dropped by an earlier oak. Every man began with the union of an ovum and a spermatozoon, but the ovum and the spermatozoon came from two fully developed human beings. The modern express engine came from the *Rocket*: but the *Rocket* came, not from something under and more elementary than itself but from something much more developed and highly organized —the mind of a man, and a man of genius. Modern art may have 'developed' from savage art. But then the very first picture of all did not 'evolve' itself: it came from something overwhelmingly greater than itself, from the mind of that man who by seeing for the first time that marks on a flat surface could be made to look like animals and men, proved himself to excel in sheer blinding genius any of the artists who have succeeded him. It may be true that if we trace back any existing civilization to its beginnings we shall find those beginnings crude and savage: but then when you look closer you usually find that these beginnings themselves come from a wreck of some earlier civilization. In other words, the apparent instances of, or analogies to, Evolution which impress the folk imagination, operate by fixing our attention on one half of the process. What we actually see all round us is a double process—the perfect 'dropping' an imperfect seed which in its turn develops to perfection. By concentrating exclusively on the record or upward movement in this cycle we seem to see 'evolution'. I am not in the least denying that organisms on this planet may have 'evolved'. But if we are to be guided by the analogy of Nature as we now know her, it would be reasonable to suppose that this evolutionary process was the second half of a long pattern —that the crude beginnings of life on this planet have themselves been 'dropped' there by a full and perfect life. The analogy may be mistaken. Perhaps Nature was once different. Perhaps the universe as a whole is quite different from those parts of it which fall under our observation. But if that is so, if there was once a dead universe which somehow made itself alive, if there was absolutely original savagery which raised itself by its own shoulder strap into civilization, then we ought to recognize that things of this sort happen no longer, that the world we are being asked to believe in is radically unlike the world we experience. In other words, all the immediate *plausibility* of the Myth has vanished. But it has vanished only because we have been thinking it will remain plausible to the imagination, and it is imagination which makes the Myth: it takes over from rational thought only what it finds convenient.

Another source of strength in the Myth is what the psychologists would call its 'ambivalence'. It gratifies equally two opposite tendencies of the mind, the tendency to denigration and the tendency to flattery. In the Myth everything is becoming everything else: in fact everything *is* everything else at an earlier or later stage of development—the later stages being always the better. This means that if you are feeling like Mencken you can 'debunk' all the respectable things by pointing out that they are 'merely' elaborations of the disreputable things. Love is 'merely' an elaboration of lust, virtue merely an elaboration of instinct, and so forth. On the one hand it also means that if you are feeling what the people call 'idealistic' you can regard all the nasty things (in yourself or your party or your nation) as being 'merely' the undeveloped forms of all the nice things: vice is only undeveloped virtue, egoism only undeveloped altruism, a little more education will set everything right.

The Myth also soothes the old wounds of our childhood. Without going as far as Freud we may yet well admit that every man has an old grudge against his father and his first teacher. The process of being brought up, however well it is done, cannot fail to offend. How pleasing, therefore, to abandon the old idea of 'descent' from our concocters in favour of the new idea of 'evolution' or 'emergence': to feel that we have risen from them as a flower from the earth, that we transcend them as Keats' gods transcended the Titans. One then gets a kind of cosmic excuse for regarding one's father as a muddling old Mima and his claims upon our gratitude or respect as an insufferable *stamenlied*. 'Out of the way, old fool: it is we who know to forge Nothung!'

The Myth also pleases those who want to sell things to us. In the old days, a man had a family carriage built for him when he got married and expected it to last all his life. Such a frame of mind would hardly suit modern manufacturers. But popular Evolutionism suits them exactly. Nothing *ought* to last. They want you to have a new car, a new radio set, a new everything every year. The new model must always be superseding the old. Madam would like the *latest* fashion. For this is evolution, this is development, this the way the universe itself is going: and 'sales-resistance' is the sin against the Holy Ghost, the *élan vital*.

Finally, modern politics would be impossible without the Myth. It arose in the Revolutionary period. But for the political ideals of that period it would never have been accepted. That explains why the Myth concentrates on Haldane's one case of biological 'progress' and ignores his ten cases of 'degeneration' If the cases of degeneration were kept in mind it would be impossible not to see that any given change in society is at least as likely to destroy the liberties and amenities we already have as to add new ones: that the danger of slipping back is at least as great as the chance of getting on: that a prudent society must spend at least as much energy on conserving what it has as on improvement. A clear knowledge of these truisms would be fatal both to the political Left and to the political Right of modern times. The Myth obscures that knowledge. Great parties have a vested interest in maintaining the Myth. We must therefore expect that it will survive in the popular press (including the ostensibly *comic* press) long after it has been expelled from educated circles. In Russia, where it has been built into the state religion, it may survive for centuries: for

> It has great allies,
> Its friends are propaganda, party cries,
> And bilge, and Man's incorrigible mind.

But that is not the note on which I would wish to end. The Myth has all these discreditable allies: but we should be far astray if we thought it had no others. As I have tried to show it has better allies too. It appeals to the same innocent and permanent needs in us which welcome Jack the Giant Killer. It gives us almost everything the imagination craves—irony, heroism, vastness, unity in multiplicity, and a tragic close. It appeals to every part of me except my reason. That is why those of us who feel that the Myth is already dead for us must not make the mistake of trying to 'debunk' it in the wrong way. We must not fancy that we are securing the modern world from something grim and dry, something that starves the soul. The contrary is the truth. It is our painful duty to wake the world from an enchantment. The real universe is probably in many respects less poetical, certainly less tidy and unified, than they had supposed. Man's rôle in it is less heroic. The danger that really hangs over him is perhaps entirely lacking in true tragic dignity. It is only in the last resort, and after all lesser poetries have been renounced and imagination sternly subjected to intellect, that we shall be able to offer them any compensation for what we intend to take away from them. That is why in the meantime we must treat the Myth with respect. It was all (on a certain level) nonsense: but a man would be a dull dog if he could not feel the thrill and charm of it. For my own part, though I believe it no longer, I shall always enjoy it as I enjoy other myths. I shall keep my Cave-Man where I keep Balder and Helen and the Argonauts: and there often re-visit him.

ON CHURCH MUSIC

I am a layman and one who can boast no musical education. I cannot even speak from the experience of a lifelong churchgoer. It follows that Church Music is a subject on which I cannot, even in the lowest degree, appear as a teacher. My place is in the witness box. If it concerns the court to know how the whole matter appears to such as I (not only *laicus* but *laicissimus*) I am prepared to give my evidence.

I assume from the outset that nothing should be done or sung or said in church which does not aim directly or indirectly either at glorifying God or edifying the people or both. A good service may of course have a cultural value as well, but that is not what it exists for; just as, in an unfamiliar landscape, a church may help me to find the points of the compass, but was not built for that purpose.

These two ends, of edifying and glorifying, seem to me to be related as follows. Whenever we edify, we glorify, but when we glorify we do not always edify. The edification of the people is an act of charity and obedience and therefore in itself a glorification of God. But it is possible for a man to glorify God in modes that do not edify his neighbour. This fact confronted the Church at an early stage in her career, in the phenomenon called 'speaking with tongues'. In 1 Corinthians xiv, St. Paul points out that the man who is inspired to speak in an unknown tongue may do very well, as far as he himself is concerned, but will not profit the congregation unless his utterance can be translated. Thus glorifying and edifying may come to be opposed.

Now at first sight to speak with unknown tongues and to sing anthems which are beyond the musical capacity of the people would seem to be very much the same kind of thing. It looks as if we ought to extend to the one the embargo which St Paul places on the other. And this would lead to the forbidding conclusion that no Church Music is legitimate except that which suits the existing taste of the people.

94

In reality, however, the parallel is not perhaps so close as it seems. In the first place, the mode after which a speech in an unknown tongue could glorify God was not, I suppose, the same as the mode after which learned music is held to do so. It is (to say the least) doubtful whether the speeches in 'tongues' claimed to glorify God by their aesthetic quality. I suppose that they glorified God firstly by being miraculous and involuntary, and secondly by the ecstatic state of mind in which the speaker was. The idea behind Church Music is very different. It glorifies God by being excellent in its own kind; almost as the birds and flowers and the heavens themselves glorify Him. In the composition and highly-trained execution of sacred music we offer our natural gifts at their highest to God, as we do also in ecclesiastical architecture, in vestments, in glass and gold and silver, in well-kept parish accounts, or the careful organization of a Social. And in the second place, the incapacity of the people to 'understand' a foreign language and their incapacity to 'understand' good music are not really the same. The first applies absolutely and equally (except for a lucky accident) to all the members of the congregation. The second is not equally present or equally incurable perhaps in any two individuals. And finally, the alternative to speech in an unknown tongue was speech in a known tongue. But in most discussions about Church Music the alternative to learned music is popular music—giving the people 'what they like' and allowing them to sing (or shout) their 'old favourites'.

It is here that the distinction between our problem and St Paul's seems to me to be the sharpest. That words in a known tongue might edify was obvious. Is it equally obvious that the people are edified by being allowed to shout their favourite hymns? I am well aware that the people like it. They equally like shouting *Auld Lang Syne* in the streets on New Year's Eve or shouting the latest music-hall song in a tap-room. To make a communal, familiar noise is certainly a pleasure to human beings. And I would not be thought to despise this pleasure. It is good for the lungs, it promotes good fellowship, it is humble and unaffected, it is in every way a wholesome, innocent thing—as wholesome and innocent as a pint of beer, a game of darts, or a dip in the sea. But is it, any more than these, a means of edification? No doubt it can be done—all these things can be done—eating can be done—to the glory of God. We have an Apostle's word for it. The perfected Christian can turn all his humblest, most secular, most economic, actions in that direction. But if this is accepted as an argument for popular hymns it will also be an argument for a good many other things. What we want to know is whether untrained communal singing is in itself any more edifying than other popular pleasures. And of this I, for one, am still wholly unconvinced. I have often heard this noise; I have sometimes contributed to it. I do not yet seem to have found any evidence that the physical and emotional exhilaration which it produces is necessarily, or often, of any religious relevance. What I, like many other laymen, chiefly desire in church are fewer, better, and shorter hymns; especially fewer.

The case for abolishing all Church Music whatever thus seems to me far stronger than the case for abolishing the difficult work of the trained choir and retaining the lusty roar of the congregation. Whatever doubts I feel about the spiritual value of the first I feel at least equally about the spiritual value of the second.

The first and most solid conclusion which (for me) emerges is that both musical parties, the High Brows and the Low, assume far too easily the spiritual value of the music they want. Neither the greatest excellence of a trained performance from the choir, nor the heartiest and most enthusiastic bellowing from the pews, must be taken to signify that any specifically religious activity is going on. It may be so, or it may not. Yet the main sense of Christendom, reformed and unreformed, would be against us if we tried to banish music from the Church. It remains to suggest, very tentatively, the ways in which it can really be pleasing to God or help to save the souls of men.

There are two musical situations on which I think we can be confident that a blessing rests. One is where a priest or an organist, himself a man of trained and delicate taste, humbly and charitably sacrifices his own (aesthetically right) desires and gives the people humbler and coarser fare than he would wish, in a belief (even, as it may be, the erroneous belief) that he can thus bring them to God. The other is where the stupid and unmusical layman humbly and patiently, and above all silently, listens to music which he cannot, or cannot fully, appreciate, in the belief that it somehow glorifies God, and that if it does not edify him this must be his own defect. Neither such a High Brow nor such a Low Brow can be far out of the way. To both, Church Music will have been a means of grace; not the music they have liked, but the music they have disliked. They have both offered, sacrificed, their taste in the fullest sense. But where the opposite situation arises, where the musician is filled with the pride of skill or the virus of emulation and looks with contempt on the unappreciative congregation, or where the unmusical, complacently entrenched in their own ignorance and conservatism, look with the restless and resentful hostility of an inferiority complex on all who would try to improve their taste—there, we may be sure, all that both offer is unblessed and the spirit that moves them is not the Holy Ghost.

These highly general reflections will not, I fear, be of much practical use to any priest or organist in devising a working compromise for a particular church. The most they can hope to do is to suggest that the problem is never a merely musical one. Where both the choir and the congregation are spiritually on the right road no insurmountable difficulties will occur. Discrepancies of taste and capacity will, indeed, provide matter for mutual charity and humility.

For us, the musically illiterate mass, the right way is not hard to discern; and as long as we stick to it, the fact that we are capable only of a confused rhythmical noise will not do very much harm, if, when we make it, we really intend the glory of God. For if that is our intention it follows of necessity that we shall be as ready to glorify Him by silence (when required) as by shouts. We shall also be aware that the power of shouting stands very low in the hierarchy of natural gifts, and that it would be better to learn to sing if we could. If any one tries to teach us we will try to learn. If we cannot learn, and if this is desired, we will shut up. And we will also try to listen intelligently. A congregation in this state will not complain if a good deal of the music they hear in church is above their heads. It is not the mere ignorance of the unmusical that really resists improvements. It is jealousy, arrogance, suspicion, and the wholly detestable species of conservatism which those vices engender. How far it may be politic (part of the wisdom of the serpent) to make concessions to the 'old guard' in a congregation, I would not like to determine. But I do not think it can be the business of the Church greatly to co-operate with the modern State in appeasing inferiority complexes and encouraging the natural man's instinctive hatred of excellence. Democracy is all very well as a political device. It must not intrude into the spiritual, or even the aesthetic, world.

The right way for the musicians is perhaps harder, and I, at any rate, can speak of it with much less confidence. But it seems to me that we must define rather carefully the way, or ways, in which music can glorify God. There is, as I hinted above, a sense in which all natural agents, even inanimate ones, glorify God continually by revealing the powers He has given them. And in that sense we, as natural agents, do the same. On that level our wicked actions, in so far as they exhibit our skill and strength, may be said to glorify God, as well as our good actions. An excellently performed piece of music, as a natural operation which reveals in a very high degree the peculiar powers given to man, will thus always glorify God whatever the intention of the performers may be. But that is a kind of glorifying which we share with 'the dragons and great deeps', with the 'frosts and snows'. What is looked for in us, as men, is another kind of glorifying, which depends on intention. How easy or how hard it may be for a whole choir to preserve that intention through all the discussions and decisions, all the corrections and disappointments, all the temptations to pride, rivalry and ambition, which precede the performance of a great work, I (naturally) do not know. But it is on the intention that all depends. When it succeeds, I think the performers are the most enviable of men; privileged while mortals to honour God like angels and, for a few golden moments, to see spirit and flesh, delight and labour, skill and worship, the natural and the supernatural, all fused into that unity they would have had before the Fall. But I must insist that no degree of excellence in the music, simply as music, can assure us that this paradisal state has been achieved. The excellence proves 'keenness'; but men can be 'keen' for natural, or even wicked, motives. The absence of keenness would prove that they lacked the right spirit; its presence does not prove that they have it. We must beware of the naïve idea that our music can 'please' God as it would please a cultivated human hearer. That is like thinking, under the old Law, that He really needed the blood of bulls and goats. To which an answer came, 'Mine are the cattle upon a thousand hills', and 'if I am hungry, I will not tell *thee*.' If God (in that sense) wanted music, He would not tell *us*. For all our offerings, whether of music or martyrdom, are like the intrinsically worthless present of a child, which a father values indeed, but values only for the intention.[1]

[[1] Before this article was written, Lewis was invited by the Rev Mr Eric Routley to become a member of the panel of the Hymn Society of Great Britain and Ireland to whom new hymns are submitted in order that their merit might be assessed. As could be expected, Lewis refused. However, his answers to the request are published (with Mr Routley's letters) as 'Correspondence with an Anglican who Dislikes Hymns', *The Presbyter*, VI, No. 2 (1948) pp. 15–20. (The two letters from Lewis, dated 16 July 1946 and 21 September 1946, are printed over the initials 'A.B.')]

HISTORICISM

'He that would fly without wings must fly in his dreams.'
—COLERIDGE

I give the name *Historicism* to the belief that men can, by the use of their natural powers, discover an inner meaning in the historical process. I say *by the use of their natural powers* because I do not propose to deal with any man who claims to know the meaning either of all history or of some particular historical event by divine revelation. What I mean by a Historicist is a man who asks me to accept his account of the inner meaning of history on the grounds of his learning and genius. If he had asked me to accept it on the grounds that it had been shown him in a vision, that would be another matter. I should have said to him nothing. His claim (with supporting evidence in the way of sanctity and miracles) would not be for me to judge. This does not mean that I am setting up a distinction, to be applied by myself, between inspired and un-inspired writers. The distinction is not between those who have and those who lack inspiration, but between those who claim and those who do not claim it. With the former I have at present no concern.

I say *an inner meaning* because I am not classifying as Historicists those who find a 'meaning' in history in any sense whatever. Thus, to find causal connections between historical events, is in my terminology the work of a historian not of a historicist. A historian, without becoming a Historicist, may certainly infer un-known events from known ones. He may even infer future events from past ones; prediction may be a folly, but it is not Historicism. He may 'interpret' the past in the sense of reconstructing it imaginatively, making us feel (as far as may be) what it was like, and in that sense what it 'meant', to a man to be a twelfth-century villein or a Roman *eques*. What makes all these activities proper to the historian is that in them the conclusions, like the premises, are historical. The mark of the Historicist, on the other hand, is that he tries to get from historical premises conclusions which are more than historical; conclusions metaphysical or theological or (to coin a word) atheo-logical. The historian and the Historicist may both say that something 'must have' happened. But *must* in the mouth of a genuine historian will refer only to a *ratio cognoscendi*: since A happened B 'must have' preceded it; if William the Bastard arrived in England he 'must have' crossed the sea. But 'must' in the mouth of a Historicist can have quite a different meaning. It may mean that events fell out as they did because of some ultimate, transcendent necessity in the ground of things.

When Carlyle spoke of history as a 'book of revelations' he was a Historicist. When Novalis called history 'an evangel' he was a Historicist. When Hegel saw in history the progressive self-manifestation of absolute spirit he was a Historicist. When a village woman says that her wicked father-in-law's paralytic stroke is 'a judgement on him' she is a Historicist. Evolutionism, when it ceases to be simply a theorem in biology and becomes a principle for interpreting the total historical process, is a form of Historicism. Keats' *Hyperion* is the epic of Historicism, and the words of Oceanus,

> 'tis the eternal law
> That first in beauty should be first in might,

are as fine a specimen of Historicism as you could wish to find.

The contention of this article is that Historicism is an illusion and that Historicists are, at the very best, wasting their time. I hope it is already clear that in criticizing Historicists I am not at all criticizing historians. It is not formally impossible that a Historicist and a historian should be the same man. But the two characters are in fact very seldom combined. It is usually theologians, philosophers and politicians who become Historicists.

Historicism exists on many levels. The lowest form of it is one that I have already mentioned: the doctrine that our calamities (or more often our neighbours' calamities) are 'judgements'; which here means divine condemnations or punishments. This sort of Historicism sometimes endeavours to support itself by the authority of the Old Testament. Some people even talk as if it were the peculiar mark of the Hebrew prophets to interpret history in this way. To that I have two replies. Firstly, the Scriptures come before me as a book claiming divine inspiration. I am not prepared to argue with the prophets. But if any man thinks that because God was pleased to reveal certain calamities as 'judgements' to certain chosen persons, he is therefore entitled to generalize and read all calamities in the same way, I submit that this is a *non sequitur*. Unless, of course, that man claims to be himself a prophet; and then I must refer his claim to more competent judges. But secondly, we must insist that such an interpretation of history was not the characteristic of ancient Hebrew religion, not the thing which sets it apart and makes it uniquely valuable. On the contrary, this is precisely what it shares with popular Paganism. To attribute calamity to the offended gods and therefore to seek out and punish the offender, is the most natural thing in the world and therefore the world-wide method. Examples such as the plague in *Iliad A* and the plague at the opening of the *Oedipus Tyrannus* come at once to mind. The distinctive thing, the precious peculiarity, of Scripture is the series of divine rebuffs which this naïve and spontaneous type of Historicism there receives; in the whole course of Jewish history, in the Book of Job, in Isaiah's suffering servant (liii), in Our Lord's answers about the disaster at Siloam (Luke xiii, 4) and the man born blind (John ix, 13). If this sort of Historicism survives, it survives in spite of Christianity. And in a vague form it certainly does survive. Some who in general deserve to be called true historians are betrayed into writing as if nothing failed or succeeded that did not somehow deserve to do so. We must guard against the emotional overtones of a phrase like 'the judgement of history'. It might lure us into the vulgarest of all vulgar errors, that of idolizing as the goddess History what manlier ages belaboured as the strumpet Fortune. That would sink us below the Christian, or even the best Pagan, level. The very Vikings and Stoics knew better.

But subtler and more cultivated types of Historicism now also claim that their view is especially congenial to Christianity. It has become a commonplace, as Fr Paul Henri lately remarked in his Deneke lecture at Oxford, to say that Judaic and Christian thought are distinguished from Pagan and Pantheistic thought precisely by the significance which they attribute to history. For the Pantheist, we are told, the content of time is simply illusion;

history is a dream and salvation consists in awaking. For the Greeks, we are told, history was a mere flux or, at best, cyclic: significance was to be sought not in Becoming but in Being. For Christianity, on the other hand, history is a story with a well-defined plot, pivoted on Creation, Fall, Redemption, and Judgement. It is indeed the divine revelation *par excellence*, the revelation which includes all other revelations.

That history in a certain sense must be all this for a Christian, I do not deny. In what sense, will be explained later. For the moment, I submit that the contrast as commonly drawn between Judaic or Christian thought on the one hand and Pagan or Pantheistic on the other is in some measure illusory. In the modern world, quite plainly, Historicism has a Pantheistic ancestor in Hegel and a materialistic progeny in the Marxists. It has proved so far a stronger weapon in our enemies' hands than in ours. If Christian Historicism is to be recommended as an apologetic weapon it had better be recommended by the maxim *fas est et ab hoste doceri* than on the ground of any supposedly inherent congeniality. And if we look at the past we shall find that the contrast works well as between Greek and Christian but not as between Christian and other types of Pagan. The Norse gods, for example, unlike the Homeric, are beings rooted in a historical process. Living under the shadow of Ragnarok they are pre-occupied with time. Odin is almost the god of anxiety: in that way Wagner's Wotan is amazingly true to the Eddaic original. In Norse theology cosmic history is neither a cycle nor a flux; it is irreversible, tragic epic marching deathward to the drum-beat of omens and prophecies. And even if we rule out Norse Paganism on the ground that it was possibly influenced by Christianity, what shall we do with the Romans? It is quite clear that they did not regard history with the indifference, or with the merely scientific or anecdotal interests, of the Greeks. They seem to have been a nation of Historicists. I have pointed out elsewhere that all Roman epic before Virgil was probably metrical chronicle;[1] and the subject was always the same—the coming-to-be of Rome. What Virgil essentially did was to give this perennial theme a new unity by his symbolical structure. The *Aeneid* puts forward,

[1 'Virgil and the Subject of Secondary Epic', *A Preface to Paradise Lost* (Oxford, 1942), pp. 32ff.]

though in mythical form, what is precisely a reading of history, an attempt to show what the *fata Jovis* were labouring to bring about. Everything is related not to Aeneas as an individual hero but to Aeneas as the Rome-bearer. This, and almost only this, gives significance to his escape from Troy, his *amour* with Dido, his descent into Hades, and his defeat of Turnus. *Tantae molis erat:* all history is for Virgil an immense parturition. It is from this Pagan source that one kind of Historicism descends to Dante. The Historicism of the *De Monarchia*, though skilfully, and of course sincerely, mortised into the Judaic and Christian framework, is largely Roman and Virgilian. St Augustine indeed may be rightly described as a Christian Historicist. But it is not always remembered that he became one in order to refute Pagan Historicism. The *De Civitate* answers those who traced the disasters of Rome to the anger of the rejected gods. I do not mean to imply that the task was uncongenial to St Augustine, or that his own Historicism is merely an *argumentum ad hominem*. But it is surely absurd to regard as specifically Christian in him the acceptance of a *terrain* which had in fact been chosen by the enemy.

The close connection which some see between Christianity and Historicism thus seems to me to be largely an illusion. There is no *prima facie* case in its favour on such grounds as that. We are entitled to examine it on its merits.

What appears, on Christian premises, to be true in the Historicist's position is this. Since all things happen either by the divine will or at least by the divine permission, it follows that the total content of time must in its own nature be a revelation of God's wisdom, justice, and mercy. In this direction we can go as far as Carlyle or Novalis or anyone else. History is, in that sense, a perpetual Evangel, a story written by the finger of God. If, by one miracle, the total content of time were spread out before me, and if, by another, I were able to hold all that infinity of events in my mind and if, by a third, God were pleased to comment on it so that I could understand it, then, to be sure, I could do what the Historicist says he is doing. I could read the meaning, discern the pattern. Yes; and if the sky fell we should all catch larks. The question is not what could be done under conditions never vouchsafed us *in via*, nor even (so far as I can remember) promised us *in patria*, but what can be done now under the real conditions.

I do not dispute that History is a story written by the finger of God. But have we the text? (It would be dull work discussing the inspiration of the Bible if no copy of it had ever been seen on earth.)

We must remind ourselves that the word *History* has several senses. It may mean the total content of time: past, present, and future. It may mean the content of the past only, but still the total content of the past, the past as it really was in all its teeming riches. Thirdly, it may mean so much of the past as is discoverable from surviving evidence. Fourthly, it may mean so much as has been actually discovered by historians working, so to speak, 'at the face', the pioneer historians never heard of by the public who make the actual discoveries. Fifthly, it may mean that portion, and that version, of the matter so discovered which has been worked up by great historical writers. (This is perhaps the most popular sense: *history* usually means what you read when you are reading Gibbon or Mommsen, or the Master of Trinity.) Sixthly, it may mean that vague, composite picture of the past which floats, rather hazily, in the mind of the ordinary educated man.

When men say that 'History' is a revelation, or has a meaning, in which of these six senses do they use the word *History*? I am afraid that in fact they are very often thinking of history in the sixth sense; in which case their talk about revelation or meaning is surely unplausible in the extreme. For 'history' in the sixth sense is the land of shadows, the home of wraiths like Primitive Man or the Renaissance or the Ancient-Greeks-and-Romans. It is not at all surprising, of course, that those who stare at it too long should see patterns. We see pictures in the fire. The more indeterminate the object, the more it excites our mythopoeic or 'esemplastic' faculties. To the naked eye there is a face in the moon; it vanishes when you use a telescope. In the same way, the meanings or patterns discernible in 'history' (Sense Six) disappear when we turn to 'history' in any of the higher senses. They are clearest for each of us in the periods he has studied least. No one who has distinguished the different senses of the word *History* could continue to think that history (in the sixth sense) is an evangel or a revelation. It is an effect of perspective.

On the other hand, we admit that history (in Sense One) is a story written by the finger of God. Unfortunately we have not got it. The claim of the practising Historicist then will stand or fall with his success in showing that history in one of the intermediate senses—the first being out of reach and the sixth useless for his purpose—is sufficiently close to history in the first sense to share its revealing qualities.

We drop, then, to history in Sense Two: the total content of past time as it really was in all its richness. This would save the Historicist if we could reasonably believe two things: first, that the formidable omission of the future does not conceal the point or meaning of the story, and, secondly, that we do actually possess history (Sense Two) up to the present moment. But can we believe either?

It would surely be one of the luckiest things in the world if the content of time up to the moment at which the Historicist is writing happened to contain all that he required for reaching the significance of total history. We ride with our backs to the engine. We have no notion what stage in the journey we have reached. Are we in Act I or Act V? Are our present diseases those of childhood or senility? If, indeed, we knew that history was cyclic we might perhaps hazard a guess at its meaning from the fragment we have seen. But then we have been told that the Historicists are just the people who do not think that history is merely cyclic. For them it is a real story with a beginning, a middle, and an end. But a story is precisely the sort of thing that cannot be understood till you have heard the whole of it. Or, if there are stories (bad stories) whose later chapters add nothing essential to their significance, and whose significance is therefore contained in something less than the whole, at least you cannot tell whether any given story belongs to that class until you have at least once read it to the end. Then, on a second reading, you may omit the dead wood in the closing chapters. I always now omit the last Book of *War and Peace*. But we have not yet read history to the end. There might be no dead wood. If it is a story written by the finger of God, there probably isn't. And if not, how can we suppose that we have seen 'the point' already? No doubt there are things we can say about this story even now. We can say it is an exciting story, or a crowded story, or a story with humorous characters in it. The one thing we must not say is what it means, or what its total pattern is.

But even if it were possible, which I deny, to see the significance of the whole from a truncated text, it remains to ask whether we have that truncated text. Do we possess even up to the present date the content of time as it really was in all its richness? Clearly not. The past, by definition, is not present. The point I am trying to make is so often slurred over by the unconcerned admission 'Of course we don't know *everything*' that I have sometimes despaired of bringing it home to other people's minds. It is not a question of failing to know everything: it is a question (at least as regards quantity) of knowing next door to nothing. Each of us finds that in his own life every moment of time is completely filled. He is bombarded every second by sensations, emotions, thoughts, which he cannot attend to for multitude, and nine-tenths of which he must simply ignore. A single second of lived time contains more than can be recorded. And every second of past time has been like that for every man that ever lived. The past (I am assuming in the Historicist's favour that we need consider only the human past) in its reality, was a roaring cataract of billions upon billions of such moments: any one of them too complex to grasp in its entirety, and the aggregate beyond all imagination. By far the greater part of this teeming reality escaped human consciousness almost as soon as it occurred. None of us could at this moment give anything like a full account of his own life for the last twenty-four hours. We have already forgotten; even if we remembered, we have not time. The new moments are upon us. At every tick of the clock, in every inhabited part of the world, an unimaginable richness and variety of 'history' falls off the world into total oblivion. Most of the experiences in 'the past as it really was' were instantly forgotten by the subject himself. Of the small percentage which he remembered (and never remembered with perfect accuracy) a smaller percentage was ever communicated even to his closest intimates; of this, a smaller percentage still was recorded; of the recorded fraction only another fraction has ever reached posterity. *Ad nos vix tenuis famae perlabitur aura.* When once we have realized what 'the past as it really was' means, we must freely admit that most—that nearly all —history (in Sense Two) is, and will remain, wholly unknown to us. And if *per impossibile* the whole were known, it would be wholly unmanageable. To know the whole of one minute in

Napoleon's life would require a whole minute of your own life. You could not keep up with it.

If these fairly obvious reflections do not trouble the Historicist that is because he has an answer. 'Of course', he replies, 'I admit that we do not know and cannot know (and, indeed, don't want to know) all the mass of trivialities which filled the past as they fill the present; every kiss and frown, every scratch and sneeze, every hiccup and cough. But we know the important facts.' Now this is a perfectly sound reply for a historian: I am not so clear that it will do for the Historicist. You will notice that we are now already a long way from history in Sense One—the total story written by the finger of God. First, we had to abandon the parts of that story which are still in the future. Now it appears we have not even got the text of those parts which we call 'past'. We have only selections; and selections which, as regards quantity, stand to the original text rather as one word would stand to all the books in the British Museum. We are asked to believe that from selections on that scale men (not miraculously inspired) can arrive at the meaning or plan or purport of the original. This is credible only if it can be shown that the selections make up in quality for what they lack in quantity. The quality will certainly have to be remarkably good if it is going to do that.

'The important parts of the past survive.' If a historian says this (I am not sure that most historians would) he means by 'importance' relevance to the particular inquiry he has chosen. Thus, if he is an economic historian, economic facts are for him important: if a military historian, military facts. And he would not have embarked on his inquiry unless he had some reason for supposing that relevant evidence existed. 'Important' facts, for him, usually do survive because his undertaking was based on the probability that the facts he calls important are to be had. Sometimes he finds he was mistaken. He admits defeat and tries a new question. All this is fairly plain sailing. But the Historicist is in a different position. When he says 'Important facts survive' he must mean by the 'important' (if he is saying anything to the purpose) that which reveals the inner meaning of History. The important parts of the past must for a Hegelian Historicist be those in which Absolute Spirit progressively manifests itself; for a Christian Historicist, those which reveal the purposes of God.

In this claim I see two difficulties. The first is logical. If history is what the Historicist says—the self-manifestation of Spirit, the story written by the finger of God, the revelation which includes all other revelations—then surely he must go to history itself to teach him what is important. How does he know beforehand what sort of events are, in a higher degree than others, self-manifestations of Spirit? And if he does not know that, how does he get his assurance that it is events of that type which manage (what a convenience!) to get recorded?

The second difficulty is obvious, if we think for a moment of the process whereby a fact about the past reaches, or fails to reach, posterity. Prehistoric pottery survives because earthenware is easy to break and hard to pulverize; prehistoric poetry has perished because words, before writing, are winged. Is it reasonable to conclude either that there was no poetry or that it was, by the Historicist's standard, less important than the pottery? Is there a discovered law by which important manuscripts survive and unimportant perish? Do you ever turn out an old drawer (say, at the break-up of your father's house) without wondering at the survival of trivial documents and the disappearance of those which everyone would have thought worth preservation? And I think the real historian will allow that the actual *detritus* of the past on which he works is very much more like an old drawer than like an intelligent epitome of some longer work. Most that survives or perishes survives or perishes by chance: that is, as a result of causes which have nothing to do either with the historian's or the Historicist's interests. Doubtless, it would be possible for God so to ordain these chances that what survives is always just what the Historicist needs. But I see no evidence that He has done so; I remember no promise that He would.

The 'literary' sources, as the historian calls them, no doubt record what their writers for some reason thought important. But this is of little use unless their standards of importance were the same as God's. This seems unlikely. Their standards do not agree with one another nor with ours. They often tell us what we do not greatly want to know and omit what we think essential. It is often easy to see why. Their standard of importance can be explained by their historical situation. So, no doubt, can ours. Standards of historical importance are themselves embedded in history. But then, by what standard can we judge whether the 'important' in some high-flying Hegelian sense has survived? Have we, apart from our Christian faith, any assurance that the historical events which we regard as momentous coincide with those which would be found momentous if God showed us the whole text and deigned to comment? Why should Genghis Khan be more important than the patience or despair of some one among his victims? Might not those whom we regard as significant figures—great scholars, soldiers, and statesmen—turn out to have their chief importance as giving occasion to states of soul in individuals whom we never heard of? I do not, of course, mean that those whom we call the great are not themselves immortal souls for whom Christ died, but that in the plot of history as a whole they might be minor characters. It would not be strange if we, who have not sat through the whole play, and who have heard only tiny fragments of the scenes already played, sometimes mistook a mere super in a fine dress for one of the protagonists.

On such a small and chance selection from the total past as we have, it seems to me a waste of time to play the Historicist. The philosophy of history is a discipline for which we mortal men lack the necessary data. Nor is the attempt always a mere waste of time: it may be positively mischievous. It encourages a Mussolini to say that 'History took him by the throat' when what really took him by the throat was desire. Drivel about superior races or immanent dialectic may be used to strengthen the hand and ease the conscience of cruelty and greed. And what quack or traitor will not now woo adherents or intimidate resistance with the assurance that his scheme is inevitable, 'bound to come', and in the direction which the world is already taking?

When I have tried to explain myself on this subject in conversation I have sometimes been met by the rejoinder: 'Because historians do not know all, will you forbid them to try to understand what they do know?' But this seems to me to miss the whole point. I have already explained in what sense historians should attempt to understand the past. They may infer unknown events from known, they may reconstruct, they may even (if they insist) predict. They may, in fact, tell me almost anything they like about history except its metahistorical meaning. And the reason is surely very plain. There are inquiries in which scanty evidence is worth using. We may not be able to get certainty, but we can get probability, and half a loaf is better than no bread. But there are other inquiries in which scanty evidence has the same value as no evidence at all. In a funny anecdote, to have heard all except the last six words in which the point lies, leaves you, as a judge of its comic merits, in the same position as the man who has heard none of it. The historian seems to me to be engaged on an inquiry of the first type; the Historicist, on one of the second. But let us take a closer analogy.

Suppose a lost Greek play of which fragments totalling six lines survive. They have survived, of course, in grammarians who quoted them to illustrate rare inflexions. That is, they survive because someone thought them important for some reason, not because they were important in the play as a play. If any one of them had dramatic importance, that is simply a lucky accident, and we know nothing about it. I do not condemn the classical scholar to produce nothing more than a bare text of the fragments any more than I condemn the historian to be a mere annalist. Let the scholar amend their corruptions and draw from them any conclusions he can about the history of Greek language, metre or religion. But let him not start talking to us about the significance of the play as a play. For that purpose the evidence before him has a value indistinguishable from zero.

The example of a defective text might be used in another way. Let us assume a mutilated MS, in which only a minority of passages are legible. The parts we can still read might be tolerable evidence for those features which are likely to be constant and evenly distributed over the whole; for example, spelling or handwriting. On such evidence a palaeographer might, without excessive boldness, hazard a guess about the character and nationality of the scribe. A literary critic would have much less chance of guessing correctly at the purport of the whole text. That is because the palaeographer deals with what is cyclic or recurrent, and the literary critic with something unique, and uniquely developing throughout. It is possible, though not likely, that all the torn or stained or missing leaves were written by a different scribe; and if they were not, it is very unlikely that he altered his graphic habits in all the passages we cannot check. But there is nothing in the world to prevent the legible line (at the bottom of a page)

Erimian was the noblest of the brothers ten

having been followed on the next and now missing page, by something like

As men believed; so false are the beliefs of men.

This provides the answer to a question which may be asked: Does my canon that historical premises should yield only historical conclusions entail the corollary that scientific premises should yield only scientific conclusions? If we call the speculations of Whitehead or Jeans or Eddington 'scienticism' (as distinct from 'science') do I condemn the scientist as much as the Historicist? I am inclined, so far as I can see my way at present, to answer No. The scientist and the historian seem to me like the palaeographer and the literary critic in my parable. The scientist studies those elements in reality which repeat themselves. The historian studies the unique. Both have a defective MS but its defects are by no means equally damaging to both. One specimen of gravitation, or one specimen of handwriting, for all we can see to the contrary, is as good as another. But one historical event, or one line of a poem, is different from another and different in its actual context from what it would be in any other context, and out of all these differences the unique character of the whole is built up. That is why, in my opinion, the scientist who becomes a scientist is in a stronger position than the historian who becomes a Historicist. It may not be very wise to conclude from what we know of the physical universe that 'God is a mathematician': it seems to me, however, much wiser than to conclude anything about His 'judgements' from mere history. *Caveas disputare de occultis Dei judiciis*, says the author of the *Imitation*. He even advises us what antidotes to use *quando haec suggerit inimicus*.

It will, I hope, be understood that I am not denying all access whatever to the revelation of God in history. On certain great events (those embodied in the creeds) we have what I believe to be divine comment which makes plain so much of their significance as we need, and can bear, to know. On other events, most of which are in any case unknown to us, we have no such comment. And it is also important to remember that we all have a certain limited, but direct, access to History in Sense One. We are allowed, indeed compelled, to read it sentence by sentence, and every sentence is labelled *Now*. I am not, of course, referring to what is commonly called 'contemporary history', the content of the newspapers. That is possibly the most phantasmal of all histories, a story written not by the hand of God but by foreign offices, demagogues, and reporters. I mean the real or primary history which meets each of us moment by moment in his own experience. It is very limited, but it is the pure, unedited, unexpurgated text, straight from the Author's hand. We believe that those who seek will find comment sufficient whereby to understand it in such degree as they need; and that therefore God is every moment 'revealed in history', that is, in what MacDonald called 'the holy present'. Where, except in the present, can the Eternal be met? If I attack Historicism it is not because I intend any disrespect to primary history, the real revelation springing direct from God in every experience. It is rather because I respect this real original history too much to see with unconcern the honours due to it lavished on those fragments, copies of fragments, copies of copies of fragments, or floating reminiscences of copies of copies, which are, unhappily, confounded with it under the general name of *history*.

THE PSALMS

The dominant impression I get from reading the Psalms is one of antiquity. I seem to be looking into a deep pit of time, but looking through a lens which brings the figures who inhabit that depth up close to my eye. In that momentary proximity they are almost shockingly alien; creatures of unrestrained emotion, wallowing in self-pity, sobbing, cursing, screaming in exultation, clashing uncouth weapons or dancing to the din of strange musical instruments. Yet, side by side with this, there is also a different image in my mind: Anglican choirs, well laundered surplices, soapy boys' faces, hassocks, an organ, prayer-books, and perhaps the smell of new-mown graveyard grass coming in with the sunlight through an open door. Sometimes the one, sometimes the other, impression grows faint, but neither, perhaps, ever quite disappears. The irony reaches its height when a boy soloist sings in that treble which is so beautifully free from all personal emotion the words whereby ancient warriors lashed themselves with frenzy against their enemies; and does this in the service of the God of Love, and himself, meanwhile, perhaps thinks neither of that God nor of ancient wars but of 'bullseyes' and the Comics. This irony, this double or treble vision, is part of the pleasure. I begin to suspect that it is part of the profit too.

How old the Psalms, as we now have them, really are is a question for the scholars. I am told there is one (No. 18) which might really have come down from the age of David himself; that is, from the tenth century B.C. Most of them, however, are said to be 'post exilic'; the book was put together when the Hebrews, long exiled in Babylonia, were repatriated by that enlightened ruler, Cyrus of Persia. This would bring us down to the sixth century. How much earlier material the book took in is uncertain. Perhaps for our present purpose it does not greatly matter. The whole spirit and technique and the characteristic attitudes in the Psalms we have might be very like those of much older sacred poetry which is now lost. We know that they had

114

such poetry; they must have been already famous for that art when their Babylonian conquerors (see No. 137) asked them for a specimen. And some very early pieces occur elsewhere in the Old Testament. Deborah's song of triumph over Sisera in Judges V might be as old as the battle that gave rise to it back in the thirteenth century. If the Hebrews were conservative in such matters then sixth century poems may be very like those of their ancestors. And we know they were conservative. One can see that by leaping forward six centuries into the New Testament and reading the *Magnificat*. The Virgin has something other (and more momentous) to say than the old Psalmists; but what she utters is quite unmistakably a psalm. The style, the dwelling on Covenant, the delight in the vindication of the poor, are all perfectly true to the old model. So might the old model have been true to one yet older. For poetry of that sort did not, like ours, seek to express those things in which individuals differ, and did not aim at novelty. Even if the Psalms we read were all composed as late as the sixth century B.C., in reading them I suspect that we have our hands on the near end of a living cord that stretches far back into the past.

In most moods the spirit of the Psalms feels to me more alien than that of the oldest Greek literature. But that is not an affair of dates. Distance in temper does not always coincide with distance in time. To most of us, perhaps to all of us at most times (unless we are either very uneducated or very holy or, as might be, both) the civilization that descends from Greece and Rome is closer, more congenial, than what we inherit from ancient Israel. The very words and concepts which we use for science, philosophy, criticism, government, grammar, are all Graeco-Roman. It is this, and not Israel, that has made us, in the ordinary sense, 'civilized'. But no Christian can read the Bible without discovering that these ancient Hebrews, generally so remote, may at any moment turn out to be our brothers in a sense in which no Greek or Roman ever was. What a dull, remote thing, for example, the Book of Proverbs seems at a first glance: bearded Orientals uttering endless platitudes as if in a parody of the *Arabian Nights*. Compared with Plato or Aristotle—compared even with Xenophon—it is not *thought* at all. Then, suddenly, just as you are going to give it up, your eye falls on the words, 'If thine enemy be hungry, give him bread to eat, and if he be thirsty give him water to drink' (xxv, 21).

One rubs one's eyes. So they were saying that already. They knew that so long before Christ came. There is nothing like it in Greek, nor, if my memory serves me, in Confucius. And this is the sort of surprise we shall often get in the Psalms. These strange, alien figures may at any moment show that, in spiritual descent (as opposed to cultural) it is they, after all, who are our ancestors and the classical nations who are alien. Conversely, in reading the classics we sometimes have the opposite surprise. Those loved authors, so civilized, tolerant, humane, and enlightened, every now and then reveal that they are divided from us by a gulf. Hence the eternal, roguish tittering about pederasty in Plato or the hard pride that makes Aristotle's *Ethics* in places almost comic. We begin to doubt whether any one of them (even Virgil himself) if we could recall him from the dead might not, in the first hour's conversation, let out something that would utterly estrange us.

I do not at all mean that the Hebrews were just 'better' than the Greeks and the Romans. On the contrary we shall find in the Psalms expressions of a cruelty more vindictive and a self-righteousness more complete than anything in the classics. If we ignore such passages and read only a few selected favourite Psalms, we miss the point. For the point is precisely this: that these same fanatic and homicidal Hebrews, and not the more enlightened peoples, again and again—for brief moments—reach a Christian level of spirituality. It is not that they are better or worse than the Pagans, but that they are both better and worse. One is forced to recognize that, in one respect, these alien poèts are our predecessors, and the only predecessors we can find in all antiquity. They have something the Pagans have not. They know something of which Socrates was ignorant. This Something does not seem to us to arise at all naturally from what else we can see of their character. It looks like something that has been given them from outside; in fact, like what it professes to be, a revelation. Their claim to be the 'Chosen' people is strong.

We may, indeed, be surprised at the choice. If we had been allowed to see the world as it was, say, in the fifteenth century B.C., and asked to guess which of the stocks then existing was going to be entrusted with the consciousness of God and with the transmission of that blood which would one day produce a body for the incarnation of God Himself, I do not think many of us would have guessed right. (I think the Egyptians would have been my own favourite.)

A similar strangeness meets us elsewhere. The raw material out of which a thing is made is not always that which would seem most promising to one who does not understand the process. There is nothing hard, brittle, or transparent about the ingredients of glass. Again, to come nearer to the present matter, do not our own personal ancestors, our family, seem at first rather improbable? Later, as we begin to recognize the heredity that works in us, we understand. But surely not at first. What young man feels 'These are exactly the sort of people whose son (or grandson, or descendant) I might be expected to be'? For usually, in early life, the people with whom one seems to have most in common, the people who share one's interests, the 'men of one's own totem', are not one's relatives, so that the idea of having been born into the wrong family is an attractive myth. (We are delighted when the hero, in *Siegfried*, forces the dwarf to confess that he is not his son.) The thing one is made out of is not necessarily like oneself (still less, like one's idea of that self) and looks at first even more unlike than it really is. It may be so with the origins of our species. The Evolutionists say we descend from 'anthropoids', creatures akin to apes. Is it (at first sight) the descent we would have chosen? If an intelligence such as ours had looked at the pre-human world and been told that one of the species then in existence was to be raised to rational and spiritual status and at last behold its Creator face to face, would he have picked the winner? Not unless it realized the importance of its hand-like paws; just as one would not guess the ingredients of glass unless one knew some chemistry. So we, because of something we do not know, are bewildered to find the ancient Hebrews 'chosen' as they were.

From this point of view there is no better psalm to begin with than No. 109. It ends with a verse which every Christian can at once make his own: the Lord is 'the prisoner's friend', standing by the poor (or friendless) to save him from unjust judges. This is one of the characteristic notes of the Psalms and one of the things for which we love them. It anticipates the temper of the *Magnificat*. It is hardly to be paralleled in Pagan literature (the Greek gods were very active in casting down the proud, but hardly in raising the humble). It will commend itself even to a modern unbeliever of good will; he may call it wishful thinking, but he will respect the wish. In a word, if we read only the last verse we should feel in full sympathy with this psalmist. But the moment we look back at what precedes that verse, he turns out to be removed from us by infinite distances; or, worse still, to be loathsomely akin to that in us which it is the main business of life to purge away. Psalm 109 is as unabashed a hymn of hate as was ever written. The poet has a detailed programme for his enemy which he hopes God will carry out. The enemy is to be placed under a wicked ruler. He is to have 'an accuser' perpetually at his side: whether an evil spirit, a 'Satan', as our Prayer Book version renders it, or merely a human accuser—a spy, an *agent provocateur*, a member of the secret police (v. 5). If the enemy attempts to have any religious life, this, far from improving his position, must make him even worse: 'let his prayer be turned into sin' (v. 6). And after his death— which had better, please, be early (v. 7)—his widow and children and descendants are to live in unrelieved misery (vv. 8–12). What makes our blood run cold, even more than the unrestrained vindictiveness, is the writer's untroubled conscience. He has no qualms, scruples, or reservations; no shame. He gives hatred free rein—encourages and spurs it on—in a sort of ghastly innocence. He offers these feelings, just as they are, to God, never doubting that they will be acceptable: turning straight from the maledictions to 'Deal thou with me, O Lord God, according unto thy Name: for sweet is thy mercy' (v. 20).

The man himself, of course, lived very long ago. His injuries may have been (humanly speaking) beyond endurance. He was doubtless a hot-blooded barbarian, more like a modern child than a modern man. And though we believe (and can even see from the last verse) that some knowledge of the real God had come to his race, yet he lived in the cold of the year, the early spring of Revelation, and those first gleams of knowledge were like snow drops, exposed to the frosts. For him, then, there may have been excuses. But we—what good can we find in reading such stuff?

One good, certainly. We have here an uninhibited expression of those feelings which oppression and injustice naturally produce. The psalm is a portrait: under it should be written 'This is what you make of a man by ill-treating him.' In a modern child or savage the results might be exactly the same. In a modern,

Western European adult—especially if he were a professing Christian—they would be more sophisticated; disguised as a disinterested love of justice, claiming to be concerned with the good of society. But under that disguise, and none the better for it in the sight of God, the feelings might still be there. (I am thinking of a total stranger who forwarded to me a letter written to her in denigration of myself by another total stranger, because, as she said, 'she felt it her duty'.) Now in a case of what we ordinarily call 'seduction' (that is, sexual seduction) we should think it monstrous to dwell on the guilt of the party who yielded to temptation and ignore that of the party who tempted. But every injury or oppression is equally a temptation, a temptation to hatred, and in that sense a seduction. Whenever we have wronged our fellow man, we have tempted him to be such a man as wrote Psalm 109. We may have repented of our wrong: we do not always know if he has repented of his hatred. How do accounts now stand between us if he has not?

I do not know the answer to that question. But I am inclined to think that we had better look unflinchingly at the sort of work we have done; like puppies, we must have 'our noses rubbed in it'. A man, now penitent, who has once seduced and abandoned a girl and then lost sight of her, had better not avert his eyes from the crude realities of the life she may now be living. For the same reason we ought to read the psalms that curse the oppressor; read them with fear. Who knows what imprecations of the same sort have been uttered against ourselves? What prayers have Red men, and Black, and Brown and Yellow, sent up against us to their gods or sometimes to God Himself? All over the earth the White Man's offence 'smells to heaven': massacres, broken treaties, theft, kidnappings, enslavement, deportation, floggings, lynchings, beatings-up, rape, insult, mockery, and odious hypocrisy make up that smell. But the thing comes nearer than that. Those of us who have little authority, who have few people at our mercy, may be thankful. But how if one is an officer in the army (or, perhaps worse, an N.C.O.)? a hospital matron? a magistrate? a prison-warden? a school prefect? a trade-union official? a Boss of any sort? in a word, anyone who cannot be 'answered back'? It is hard enough, even with the best will in the world, to be just. It is hard, under the pressure of haste, uneasiness, ill-temper, self-complacency, and conceit, even to continue intending justice. Power corrupts; the 'insolence of office' will creep in. We see it so clearly in our superiors; is it unlikely that our inferiors see it in us? How many of those who have been over us did not sometimes (perhaps often) need our forgiveness? Be sure that we likewise need the forgiveness of those that are under us.

We may not always receive it. They may not be Christians at all. They may not be far enough on the way to master that hard work of forgiveness which we have set them. Bitter, chronic resentment, unsuccessfully resisted or not resisted at all, may be burning against us: the spirit, essentially, of Psalm 109.

I do not mean that God hears and will grant such prayers as that psalmist uttered. They are wicked. He condemns them. All resentment is sin. And we may hope that those things which our inferiors resent were not really half so bad as they imagine. The snub was unintentional; the high-handed behaviour on the bench was due to ignorance and an uneasy awareness of one's own incapacity; the seemingly unfair distribution of work was not really unfair, or not intended to be; the inexplicable personal dislike for one particular inferior, so obvious to him and to some of his fellows, is something of which we are genuinely unconscious (it appears in our conscious mind as discipline, or the need for making an example). Anyway, it is very wicked of of them to hate us. Yes; but the folly consists in supposing that God sees the wickedness in them apart from the wickedness in us which provoked it. They sin by hatred because we tempted them. We have, in that sense, seduced, debauched them. They are, as it were, the mothers of this hatred: we are the fathers.

It is from this point of view that the *Magnificat* is terrifying. If there are two things in the Bible which should make our blood run cold, it is one; the other is that phrase in Revelation, 'The wrath of the lamb'. If there is not mildness in the Virgin Mother, if even the lamb, the helpless thing that bleats and has its throat cut, is not the symbol of the harmless, where shall we turn? The resemblance between the *Magnificat* and traditional Hebrew poetry which I noted above is no mere literary curiosity. There is, of course, a difference. There are no cursings here, no hatred, no self-righteousness. Instead, there is mere statement. He has scattered the proud, cast down the mighty, sent the rich empty away. I spoke just now of the ironic contrast between the fierce psalmists and the choir-boy's treble. The contrast is here brought up to a higher level. Once more we have the treble voice, a girl's voice, announcing without sin that the sinful prayers of her ancestors do not remain entirely unheard; and doing this, not indeed with fierce exultation, yet—who can mistake the tone?—in a calm and terrible gladness.

I am tempted here to digress for a moment into a speculation which may bring ease to us in one direction while it alarms us in another. Christians are unhappily divided about the kind of honour in which the Mother of the Lord should be held, but there is one truth about which no doubt seems admissible. If we believe in the Virgin Birth and if we believe in Our Lord's human nature, psychological as well as physical (for it is heretical to think Him a human body which had the Second Person of the Trinity *instead of* a human soul) we must also believe in a human heredity for that human nature. There is only one source for it (though in that source all the true Israel is summed up). If there is an iron element in Jews may we not without irreverence guess whence, humanly speaking, it came? Did neighbours say, in His boyhood, 'He's His Mother's Son'? This might set in a new and less painful light the severity of some things He said to, or about, His Mother. We may suppose that she understood them very well.

I have called this a digression, but I am not sure that it is one. Two things link the Psalms with us. One is the *Magnificat*, and one, Our Lord's continued quotations from them, though not, to be sure, from such Psalms as 109. We cannot reject from our minds a book in which His was so steeped. The Church herself has followed Him and steeped our minds in the same book.

In a word, the Psalmists and we are both in the Church. Individually they, like us, may be sometimes very bad members of it; tares, but tares that we have no authority to pull up. They may often be ignorant, as we (though perhaps in different ways) are ignorant, what spirit they are of. But we cannot excommunicate them, nor they us.

I do not at all mean (though if you watch, you will certainly find some critic who says I meant) that we are to make any concession to their ferocity. But we may learn to see the good thing which that ferocity is mixed with. Through all their excesses there runs a passionate craving for justice. One is tempted at first to say that such a craving, on the part of the oppressed, is no very great merit; that the wickedest men will cry out for fair play when you give them foul play. But unfortunately this is not true. Indeed at this very moment the spirit which cries for justice may be dying out.

Here is an alarming example. I had a pupil who was certainly a socialist, probably a Marxist. To him the 'collective', the State, was everything, the individual nothing; freedom, a bourgeois delusion. Then he went down and became a schoolmaster. A couple of years later, happening to be in Oxford, he paid me a visit. He said he had given up socialism. He was completely disillusioned about state-control. The interferences of the Ministry of Education with schools and schoolmasters were, he had found, arrogant, ignorant, and intolerable: sheer tyranny. I could take lots of this and the conversation went on merrily. Then suddenly the real purpose of his visit was revealed. He was so 'browned-off' that he wanted to give up schoolmastering; and could I—had I any influence—would I pull any wires to get him a job—*in the Ministry of Education*?

There you have the new man. Like the psalmists he can hate, but he does not, like the psalmists, thirst for justice. Having decided that there is oppression he immediately asks: 'How can I join the oppressors?' He has no objection to a world which is divided between tyrants and victims; the important thing is which of these two groups you are in. (The moral of the story remains the same whether you share his view about the Ministry or not.)

There is, then, mixed with the hatred in the psalmists, a spark which should be fanned, not trodden out. That spark God saw and fanned, till it burns clear in the *Magnificat*. The cry for 'judgement' was to be heard.

But the ancient Hebrew idea of 'judgement' will need an essay to itself.

II

The Day of Judgement is an idea very familiar, and very dreadful, to Christians. 'In all times of our tribulation, in all time of our wealth, in the hour of death, and in the day of judgement, Good Lord deliver us.' If there is any concept which cannot by any conjuring be removed from the teaching of Our Lord, it is that of the great separation; the sheep and the goats, the broad way and the narrow, the wheat and the tares, the winnowing fan, the wise and foolish virgins, the good fish and the refuse, the door closed on the marriage feast, with some inside and some outside in the dark. We may dare to hope—some dare to hope—that this is not the whole story, that, as Julian of Norwich said, 'All will be well and all manner of thing will be well.' But it is no use going to Our Lord's own words for that hope. Something we may get from St Paul: nothing, of that kind, from Jesus. It is from His own words that the picture of 'Doomsday' has come into Christianity.

One result of this is that the word 'judgement' in a religious context immediately suggests to us a criminal trial; the Judge on the bench, the accused in the dock, the hope of acquittal, the fear of conviction. But to the ancient Hebrews 'judgement' usually suggested something quite different.

In the Psalms judgement is not something that the conscience-stricken believer fears but something the downtrodden believer hopes for. God 'shall judge the world in righteousness' and 'be a defence for the oppressed' (ix, 8-9). 'Judge me, O Lord', cries the poet of Psalm 35. More surprisingly, in 67 even the 'nations', the Gentiles, are told to 'rejoice and be glad' because God will 'judge the folk righteously'. (Our fear is precisely lest the judgement should be a good deal more righteous than we can bear.) In the jubilant 96th Psalm the very sky and earth are to 'be glad', the fields are to 'be joyful' and all the trees of the wood 'shall rejoice before the Lord' because 'He cometh to judge the earth'. At the prospect of that judgement which we dread there is such revelry as a Pagan poet might have used to herald the coming of Dionysus.

Though our Lord, as I have said, imposed on us the modern, Christian conception of the Day of Judgement, yet His own words elsewhere illuminate the old Hebraic conception. I am thinking of the Unjust Judge in the parable. To most of us, unless we had that parable in mind, the mention of a wicked judge would instantly suggest someone like Judge Jeffries: a roaring, interrupting, bloodthirsty brute, bent on hanging a prisoner, bullying the jury and the witnesses. Our hope is that we shall *not* be judged by him. Our Lord's Unjust Judge is a wholly different character. You want him to judge you, you pester him to judge you. The whole difficulty is to get your case heard. Obviously what Our Lord has in view is not a criminal trial at all but a civil trial. We are looking at 'justice' from the point of view not of a prisoner but of a plaintiff: a plaintiff with a watertight case, if only she could get the defendant into court.

The picture is strange to us only because we enjoy in our own country an unusually good legal profession. We take it for granted that judges do not need to be bribed and cannot be bribed. This is, however, no law of nature, but a rare achievement; we ourselves might lose it (shall certainly lose it if no pains are taken for its conservation); it does not inevitably go with the use of the English language. Over many parts of the world and in many periods the difficulty for poor and unimportant people has been not only to get their case fairly heard but to get it heard at all. It is their voices that speak in the continual hope of the Hebrews for 'judgement', the hope that some day, somehow, wrongs will be righted.

But the idea is not associated only with courts of law. The 'Judges' who give their name to a most interesting historical book in the Old Testament were not, I gather, so called only because they sometimes exercised what we should consider judicial functions. Indeed the book has very little to say about 'judging' in that sense. Its 'judges' are primarily heroes, fighting men, who deliver Israel from foreign tyrants: giant-killers. The name which we translate as 'judges' is apparently connected with a verb which means to vindicate, to avenge, to right the wrongs of. They might equally well be called champions, avengers. The knight errant of medieval romance who spends his days liberating, and securing justice for, distressed damsels, would almost have been, for the Hebrews, a 'judge'.

Such a Judge—He who will at last do us right, the deliverer, the protector, the queller of tyrants—is the dominant image in the Psalms. There are, indeed, some few passages in which a psalmist thinks of 'judgement' with trembling: 'Enter not into judgement with thy servant: for in thy sight shall no man living be justified' (143, 2), or 'If thou, Lord, wilt be extreme to mark what is done amiss: O Lord, who may abide it?' (130, 3). But the opposite attitude is far commoner: 'Hear the right, O Lord' (17, 1), 'Be thou my Judge' (26, 1), 'Plead thou my cause' (35, 1), 'Give sentence with me, O God' (43, 1), 'Arise, thou Judge of the world' (94, 2). It is for justice, for a hearing, far more often than for pardon, that the psalmists pray.

We thus reach a very paradoxical generalization. Ordinarily, and of course correctly, the Jewish and the Christian church, the reign of Moses and the reign of Christ, are contrasted as Law against Grace, justice against mercy, rigour against tenderness. Yet apparently those who live under the sterner dispensation hope for God's judgement while those who live under the milder fear it. How does this come about? The answer, by and large, will be plain to all who have read the Psalms with attention. The psalmists, with very few exceptions, are eager for judgement because they believe themselves to be wholly in the right. Others have sinned against them; their own conduct (as they frequently assure us) has been impeccable. They earnestly invite the divine inspection, certain that they will emerge from it with flying colours. The adversary may have things to hide, but they have not. The more God examines their case, the more unanswerable it will appear. The Christian, on the other hand, trembles because he knows he is a sinner.

Thus in one sense we might say that Jewish confidence in the face of judgement is a by-product of Jewish self-righteousness. But that is far too summary. We must consider the whole experience out of which the self-righteous utterances grow: and secondly, what, on a deeper level, those utterances really mean.

The experience is dark and dreadful. We must not call it the 'dark night of the soul' for that name is already appropriate to another darkness and another dread, encountered at a far higher level than (I suppose) any of the psalmists had reached. But we may well call it the Dark Night of the Flesh, understanding by 'the flesh' the natural man. For the experience is not in itself necessarily religious and thousands of unbelievers undergo it in our own time. It arises from natural causes; but it becomes religious in the psalmists because they are religious men.

It must be confessed at the outset that all those passages which paint this Dark Night can be regarded, if we wish, as the expressions of a neurosis. If we choose to maintain that several psalmists wrote in, or on the verge of, a nervous breakdown, our theory will cover all the facts. That is, the psalmists assert as true about their own situation all those things which a patient, in a certain neurotic condition, wrongly believes to be true of his. For our present purpose, I think this does not matter much. Neurosis is a thing that occurs; we may have passed, or may yet have to pass, through that valley. It concerns us to see how certain believers in God behaved in it before us. And neurosis is, after all, a relative term. Who can say that he never touches the fringes of it? Even if the Psalms were written by neurotics, that will not make them wholly irrelevant.

But of course we cannot be at all sure that they were. The neurotic wrongly believes that he is threatened by certain evils. But another man (or the neurotic himself at another time) may be really threatened with those same evils. It may be only the patient's nerves that make him so sure that he has cancer, or is financially ruined, or is going to hell; but this does not prove that there are no such things as cancer or bankruptcy or damnation. To suggest that the situation described in certain psalms must be imaginary seems to me to be wishful thinking. The situation does occur in real life. If anyone doubts this let him consider, while I try to present this Dark Night of the Flesh, how easily it might be, not the subjective impression, but the real situation of any one of the following:

1. A small, ugly, unathletic, unpopular boy in his second term at a thoroughly bad English public school. 2. An unpopular recruit in an army hut. 3. A Jew in Hitler's Germany. 4. A man in a bad firm or government office whom a group of rivals are trying to get rid of. 5. A Papist in sixteenth-century England. 6. A Protestant in sixteenth-century Spain. 7. An African in Malan's Africa. 8. An American socialist in the hands of Senator McCarthy or a Zulu, noxious to Chaka, during one of the old, savage witch-hunts.

The Dark Night of the Flesh can be objective; it is not even very uncommon.

One is alone. The fellow-recruit who seemed to be a friend on the first day, the boys who were your friends last term, the neighbours who were your friends before the Jew-baiting began (or before you attracted Senator McCarthy's attention), even your connections and relatives, have begun to give you a wide berth. No one wishes to be seen with you. When you pass acquaintances in the street they always happen to be looking the other way. 'They of mine acquaintance were afraid of me; and they that did see me without conveyed themselves from me' (31, 13). Lovers, neighbours, kinsmen stand 'afar off' (38, 11). 'I am become a stranger unto my brethren' (69, 8). 'Thou hast put away mine acquaintance far from me: and made me to be abhorred of them' (88, 7). 'I looked also upon my right hand and saw there was no man that would know me' (142, 4).

Sometimes it is not an individual but a group (a religious body or even a whole nation) that has this experience. Members fall off; allies desert; the huge combinations against us extend and harden daily. Harder even to bear than our dwindling numbers and growing isolation, is the increasing evidence that 'our side' is ineffective. The world is turned upside down by bad men and 'What hath the righteous done?', where are our counter-measures? (11, 3). We are 'put to rebuke' (12, 9). Once there were omens in our favour and great leaders on our side. But those days are gone: 'We see not our tokens, there is not one prophet more' (74, 10). England in modern Europe and Christians in modern England often feel like this.

And all round the isolated man, every day, is the presence of the unbelievers. They know well enough what we are believing or trying to believe ('help thou my unbelief') and regard it as total illusion. 'Many one there be that say of my soul, There is no help for him in his God' (3, 2). As if God, supposing He exists, had nothing to do but look after *us*! (10, 14); but in fact, 'There is no God' (14, 1). If the sufferer's God really exists 'let Him deliver him' now! (22, 8). 'Where is now thy God?' (42, 3).

The man in the Dark Night of the Flesh is in everyone else's eyes extremely funny; the stock joke of that whole school or hut or office. They can't see him without laughing: they make faces at him (22, 7). The drunks work his name into their comic songs (69, 12). He is a 'by-word' (44, 15). Unfortunately all this laughter is not exactly honest, spontaneous laughter such as a man with some oddity of voice or face might learn to bear and even, in the end, to join in. These mockers do not laugh *although* it hurts him nor even without caring whether it hurts or not; they laugh *because* it will hurt. Any humiliation or miscarriage of his is jam to them; they crow over him when he's down—'when my foot slipped, they rejoiced greatly against me' (38, 16).

If one had a certain sort of aristocratic and Stoic pride one might perhaps answer scorn with scorn and even (in a sense) rejoice, as Coventry Patmore rejoiced, to live 'in the high mountain air of public obloquy'. If so, one would not be completely in the Dark Night. But the sufferer, for better or worse, is not—or if he once was, is now no longer—that sort of man. The continual taunts, slights, and humiliations (partly veiled or brutally plain according to the *milieu*) get past his defences and under his skin. He is in his own eyes also the object they would make him. He has no come-back. Shame has covered his face (69, 7). He might as well be a dumb man; in his mouth are no reproofs (38, 13). He is 'a worm and no man' (22, 6).

THE LANGUAGE OF RELIGION

I have been asked to talk about religious language and the gist of what I have to say is that, in my opinion, there is no specifically religious language. I admit of course that some things said by religious people can't be treated exactly as we treat scientific statements. But I don't think that is because they are specimens of some special language. It would be truer to say that the scientific statements are in a special language. The language of religion, which we may presently have to distinguish from that of theology, seems to me to be, on the whole, either the same sort we use in ordinary conversation or the same sort we use in poetry, or somewhere between the two. In order to make this clearer, I am afraid I must turn away from the professed subject of my paper for some time and talk about language

I begin with three sentences (1) It was very cold (2) There were 13 degrees of frost (3) 'Ah, bitter chill it was! The owl, for all his feathers was a-cold; The hare limped trembling through the frozen grass, And silent was the flock in woolly fold: Numb'd were the Beadsman's fingers.' I should describe the first as Ordinary language, the second as Scientific language, and the third as Poetic language. Of course there is no question here of different languages in the sense in which Latin and Chinese are different languages. Two and three are improved uses of the same language used in one. Scientific and Poetic language are two different artificial perfections of Ordinary: artificial, because they depend on skills; different, because they improve Ordinary in two different directions. Notice also that Ordinary could advance a little towards either so that you could pass by degrees into Scientific or Poetic. For 'very cold' you could substitute 'freezing hard' and, for 'freezing hard', 'freezing harder than last night'. That would be getting nearer to the Scientific. On the other hand you could say 'bitterly cold' and then you would be getting nearer the Poetic. In fact you would have anticipated one of the terms used in Keats's description.

The superiority of the Scientific description clearly consists in giving for the coldness of the night a precise quantitative estimate which can be tested by an instrument. The test ends all disputes. If the statement survives the test, then various inferences can be drawn from it with certainty: e.g., various effects on vegetable and animal life can be predicted. It is therefore of use in what Bacon calls 'operation'. We can take action on it. On the other hand it does not, of itself, give us any information about the quality of a cold night, does not tell us what we shall be feeling if we go out of doors. If, having lived all our lives in the tropics, we didn't know what a hard frost was like, the thermometer reading would not of itself inform us. Ordinary language would do that better—'Your ears will ache'—'You'll lose the feeling in your fingers'—'You'll feel as if your ears were coming off.' If I could tell you (which unhappily I can't) the temperature of the coldest water I ever bathed in, it would convey the reality only to the few who had bathed in many temperatures and taken thermometer readings of them. When I tell you 'It was so cold that at first it felt like scalding hot water', I think you will get a better idea of it. And where a scientific statement could draw on no experience at all, like statements about optics made to a student born blind, then, though it might retain its proper virtues of precision, verifiability, and use in operation, it would in one sense convey nothing. Only in one sense, of course. The blind student could, presumably, draw inferences from it and use it to gain further knowledge.

I now turn to the Poetic. Its superiority to Ordinary language is, I am afraid, a much more troublesome affair. I feel fairly sure what it does not consist in: it does not consist either in discharging or arousing more emotion. It may often do one of these things or both, but I don't think that is its *differentia*. I don't think our bit of Keats differs from the Ordinary 'It was very cold' primarily or solely by getting off Keats's chest more dislike of cold nights, nor by arousing more dislike in me. There is, no doubt, some mere 'getting off the chest' in the exclamation 'Ah' and the catachresis 'bitter'. Personally, I don't feel the emotion to be either Keats's or mine. It is for me the imagined people in the story who are saying 'Ah' and 'bitter'; not with the result of making me share their discomfort, but of making me imagine how very cold it was. And the rest is all taken up with pictures of what might have been observed on such a night. The invitation is not to my emotions but to my senses. Keats seems to me to be simply conveying the quality of a cold night, and not imposing any emotions on me (except of course the emotion of pleasure at finding anything vividly conveyed to the imagination). He is in fact giving me all that concrete, qualitative information which the Scientific statement leaves out. But then, of course, he is not verifiable, nor precise, nor of much use for operation.

We must not, however, base our view on a single passage, which may have been unfairly chosen. Let us begin at quite another point. One of the most obvious differences between all the poetry I have ever read and all the straight prose (I say 'straight' to exclude prose which verges on the poetic) is this simple one, hardly ever stated: the poetry contains a great many more adjectives. This is perfectly obvious. From Homer, who never omits to tell us that the ships were black and the sea salt, or even wet, down to Eliot with his 'hollow valley' and 'multi-foliate rose', they all do it. Poets are always telling us that grass is green, or thunder loud, or lips red. It is not, except in bad poets, always telling us that things are shocking or delightful. It does not, in that direct way, attempt to discharge or excite emotion. On the contrary, it seems anxious to bombard us with masses of factual information which we might, on a prose view, regard as irrelevant or platitudinous.

[Here pages 4 and 5 of the manuscript are missing. Page 6 begins as follows:]

[In order to] discharge an emotion it is not necessary that we should make it clear to any audience. By 'expression' I mean that sort of utterance which will make clear to others how we are feeling. There are, of course, any number of intermediate stages between discharge and expression: but perfect expression in the presence of the perfect hearer would enable him to know exactly how you were feeling. To what extent this involves arousing the same emotion, or a replica of it in him—in other words, to what extent the perfect expression would be emotive—I don't know. But I think that to respond to expression is in principle different from having an emotion aroused in one, even though the arousing of some sort of phantom emotion may always be involved. There seems to me to be a difference between understanding another person's fear because he has expressed it well and being actually *infected* by his fear as so often happens. Or again, there seems to be a difference between understanding the feelings of Shakespeare's Troilus before his assignation and being infected by similar feelings, as the writer of pornography intends to infect us.

But the really important point is the third[1] one. Even if Poetic language often expresses emotion and thereby (to some undefined extent) arouses emotion, it does not follow that the expression of emotion is always its sole, or even its chief function. For even in Ordinary language one of the best ways of describing something is to tell what reactions it provoked in us. If a man says, 'They kept their rooms terribly over-heated. Before I'd been in there five minutes, I was dripping', he is usually not concerned, as an end in itself, with giving us autobiographical fact that he perspired. He wants to make us realize how hot it was. And he takes the right way. Indeed in the last resort there is hardly any other way. To say that things were blue, or hard, or cool, or foul-smelling, or noisy, is to tell how they affected our senses. To say that someone is a bore, or a decent chap, or revolting, is to tell how he affected our emotions. In the same way, I think that Poetic language often expresses emotion not for its own sake but in order to inform us about the object which aroused the emotion. Certainly it seems to me to give us such information. Burns tells us that a woman is like a red, red rose, and Wordsworth that another woman is like a violet by a mossy stone half hidden from the eye. Now of course the one woman resembles a rose, and the other a half-hidden violet, not in size, weight, shape, colour, anatomy, or intelligence, but by arousing emotions in some way analogous to those which the flowers would arouse. But then we know quite well what sort of women (and how different from each other) they must have been to do so. The two statements do not in the least reduce to mere expressions of admiration. They tell us what kind of admiration and therefore what kind of woman. They are even, in their own proper way, verifiable or

[1 Apparently referring to an enumeration of points Lewis made in the missing pages.]

falsifiable: having seen the two women we might say 'I see what he meant in comparing her to a rose' and 'I see what he meant in comparing her to a violet', or might decide that the comparisons were bad. I am not of course denying that there are other love poems (some of Wyatt's, for example) where the poet is wholly concerned with his own emotions and we get no impression of the woman at all. I deny that this is the universal rule.

Finally we have those instances where Poetic language expresses an experience which is not accessible to us in normal life at all, an experience which the poet himself may have imagined and not, in the ordinary sense, 'had'. An instance would be when Asia, in *Prometheus Unbound*, says 'My soul is an enchanted boat.' If anyone thinks this is only a more musical and graceful way of saying 'Gee! this is fine', I disagree with him. An enchanted boat moves without oar or sail to its destined haven. Asia is at that moment undergoing a process of transfiguration, almost of apotheosis. Effortless and unimpeded movement to a goal desired but not yet seen is the point. If we were experiencing Asia's apotheosis we should feel like that. In fact we have never experienced apotheosis. Nor, probably, has Shelley. But to communicate the emotion which would accompany it is to make us know more fully than before what we meant by apotheosis.

This is the most remarkable of the powers of Poetic language: to convey to us the quality of experiences which we have not had, or perhaps can never have, to use factors within our experience so that they become pointers to something outside our experience —as two or more roads on a map show us where a town that is off the map must lie. Many of us have never had an experience like that which Wordsworth records near the end of *Prelude* XIII; but when he speaks of 'the visionary dreariness' I think we get an inkling of it. Other examples would be (for me) Marvell's 'green thought in a green shade', and (for everyone) Pope's 'die of a rose in aromatic pain'. Perhaps the most astonishing is in the *Paradiso* where Dante says that as he rose from one sphere of the Ptolemaic universe to the next, he knew that he had risen only by finding that he was moving forward more quickly.[1]

It must be remembered that I have been speaking simply of

[1 I cannot find this in the *Paradiso*. It may be, however, a conflation of several passages. See *Paradiso* viii, 13; x, 35; and xiv, 85.]

Poetic language not of poetry. Poetry of course has other characteristics besides its language. One of them is that it is very often
fiction; it tells about people who never really lived and events
that never really took place. Hence Plato's jibe that the poets are
liars. But surely it would be a great confusion to attach the note
of fiction to every specimen of Poetic *language*. You just can't tell
whether Keats's description is of a winter night that really occurred or of one he imagined. The use of language in conveying
the quality of a real place, a person, or thing is the same we should
need to convey the quality of a feigned one.

My long, and perhaps tedious, digression on Poetic language
is now almost at an end. My conclusion is that such language is
by no means merely an expression, nor a stimulant, of emotion,
but a real medium of information. Which information may, like
any other, be true or false: true as Mr Young[1] on weirs, or false
as the bit in *Beowulf* about the dragon sniffing along the path.
It often does stimulate emotion, by expressing emotion, but
usually in order to show us the object to which such emotion
would be the response. A poet, Mr Robert Conquest, has put
something like my view:

> Observation of real events includes the observer, 'heart' and all;
> (The common measurable features are obtained by omitting this
> part.)
> But there is also a common aspect in the emotional
> Shared by other members of the species; this is conveyed by 'art'.
> The poem combines all these . . .[2]

Because events, as real events 'really' are and feigned events
would 'really' be if they occurred, cannot be conveyed without
bringing in the observer's heart and the common emotional
reaction of the species, it has been falsely concluded that poetry
represented the heart for its own sake, and nothing but the heart.

[1 Lewis is referring, I believe, to the Rev Canon Andrew Young, whose
poems, he felt, were something like a combination of Wordsworth and
Marvell. An interesting reference to "weirs" is found in Young's poem, "The
Slow Race". For discussion on other possibilities see my letter, "A C. S. Lewis
Mystery", *Spectator* (28 October 1966), p. 546.]

[2 'Excerpts from a Report to the Galactic Council', *The Listener*, vol. LII
(14 October 1954), p. 612.]

But I must not go too far. I think Poetic language does convey information, but it suffers from two disabilities in comparison with Scientific. (1) It is verifiable or falsifiable only to a limited degree and with a certain fringe of vagueness. Not all men, only men of some discrimination, would agree, on seeing Burn's mistress that the image of 'a red, red rose' was good, or (as might be) bad. In that sense, Scientific statements are, as people say now, far more easily 'cashed'. But the poet might of course reply that it always will be easier to cash a cheque for 30 shillings than one for 1,000 pounds, that the scientific statements are cheques, in one sense, for very small amounts, giving us, out of the teeming complexity of every concrete reality only 'the common measurable features'. (2) Such information as Poetic language has to give can be received only if you are ready to meet it half-way. It is no good holding a dialetical pistol to the poet's head and demanding how the deuce a river could have hair, or thought be green, or a woman a red rose. You may win, in the sense of putting him to a *non-plus*. But if he had anything to tell you, you will never get it by behaving in that way. You must begin by trusting him. Only by so doing will you find out whether he is trustworthy or not. *Credo ut intelligam* (it is time some theological expression came in) is here the only attitude.

Now, as I see it, the language in which we express our religious beliefs and other religious experiences, is not a special language, but something that ranges between the Ordinary and the Poetical. But even when it begins by being Ordinary, it can usually, under dialetical pressure, be found to become either Theological or Poetical. An example will best show what I mean by this trichotomy. I think the words 'I believe in God' are Ordinary language. If you press us by asking what we mean, we shall probably have to move in one of two directions. We might say 'I believe in incorporeal entity, personal in the sense that it can be the subject and object of love, on which all other entities are unilaterally dependent.' That is what I call Theological language, though far from a first-class specimen of it. In it we are attempting, so far as is possible, to state religious matter in a form more like that we use for scientific matter. This is often necessary, for purposes of instruction, clarification, controversy and the like. But it is not the language religion naturally speaks. We are applying precise, and therefore abstract, terms to what for us is the supreme example of the concrete. If we do not always feel this fully, that, I think, is because nearly all who say or read such sentences (including unbelievers) really put into them much that they know from other sources—tradition, literature, etc. But for that, it would hardly be more information than 'There are 15 degrees of frost' would be to those who had never experienced frost.

And this is one of the great disadvantages under which the Christian apologist labours. Apologetics is controversy. You cannot conduct a controversy in those poetical expressions which alone convey the concrete: you must use terms as definable and univocal as possible, and these are always abstract. And this means that the thing we are really talking about can never appear in the discussion at all. We have to try to prove *that* God is in circumstances where we are denied every means of conveying *who* God is. It is faintly parallel to the state of a witness who has to try to convey something so concrete as the known character of a friend under cross-examination. Under other conditions he might possibly succeed in giving you a real impression of him; but not under hostile cross-examination. You remember Hamlet's speech to Horatio, 'Horatio thou art e'en as just a man', etc. But you could never have had it in a witness-box.

That, then, is one way in which we could go on from 'I believe in God'—the Theological: in a sense, alien to religion, crippling, omitting nearly all that really matters, yet, in spite of everything, sometimes successful.

On the other hand, you could go on, following the spontaneous tendency of religion, into poetical language. Asked what you meant by God, you might say 'God is love' or 'the Father of lights', or even 'underneath are the everlasting arms'. From what has gone before, you will understand that I do not regard these poetical expressions as merely expressions of emotion. They will of course express emotion in any who utters them, and arouse emotion in any who hears them with belief. But so would the sentence 'Fifty Russian divisions landed in the South of England this morning.' Momentous matter, if believed, will arouse emotion whatever the language. Further, these statements make use of emotion, as Burns makes use of our emotions about roses. All this is, in my view, consistent with their being essentially informative. But, of course, informative only to those who will meet them half way.

The necessity for such poetic expressions is closely connected with the grounds on which they are believed. They are usually two: authority, and religious experience.

Christians believe that Jesus Christ is the Son of God because He said so. The other evidence about Him has convinced them that He was neither a lunatic nor a quack. Now of course the statement cannot mean that He stands to God in the very same physical and temporal relation which exists between offspring and male parent in the animal world. It is then a poetical statement. And such expression must here be necessary because the reality He spoke of is outside our experience. And here once more the religious and the theological procedure diverge. The theologian will describe it as 'analogical', drawing our minds at once away from the subtle and sensitive exploitations of imagination and emotion with which poetry works to the clear-cut but clumsy analogies of the lecture-room. He will even explain in what respects the father–son relationship is *not* analogical to the reality, hoping by elimination to reach the respects in which it is. He may even supply other analogies of his own—the lamp and the light which flows from it, or the like. It is all unavoidable and necessary for certain purposes. But there is some death in it. The sentence 'Jesus Christ is the Son of God' cannot be all got into the form 'There is between Jesus and God an asymmetrical, social, harmonious relation involving homogeneity.' Religion takes it differently. A man who is both a good son and a good father, and who is continually urged to become a better son and a better father by meditation on the Divine Fatherhood and Sonship, and who thus comes in the end to make that Divine relation the norm to which his own human sonship and fatherhood are still merely analogical, is best receiving the revelation. It would be idle to tell such a man that the formula 'is the Son of God' tells us (what is almost zero) that an unknown X is in an unknown respect 'like' the relation of father and son. He has met it half way. Information has been given him: as far as I can see, in the only way possible.

Secondly, there is religious experience, ranging from the most ordinary experiences of the believer in worship, forgiveness, dereliction, and divine help, up to the highly special experiences of the mystics. Through such experience Christians believe that they get a sort of verification (or perhaps sometimes falsification) of their tenets. Such experience cannot be conveyed to one another, much less to unbelievers, except by language which shares to some extent the nature of Poetic language. That is what leads some people to suppose that it can be nothing but emotion. For of course, if you accept the view that Poetic language is purely emotional, then things which can be expressed only in Poetic language will presumably be emotions. But if we don't equate Poetic language with emotional language, the question is still open.

Now it seems to me a mistake to think that our experience in general can be communicated by precise and literal language and that there is a special class of experiences (say, emotions) which cannot. The truth seems to me the opposite: there is a special region of experiences which can be communicated *without* Poetic language, namely, its 'common measurable features', but most experience cannot. To be incommunicable by Scientific language is, so far as I can judge, the normal state of experience. All our sensuous experience is in this condition, though this is somewhat veiled from us by the fact that much of it is very common and therefore everyone will understand our references to it at a hint. But if you have to describe to a doctor any unusual sensation, you will soon find yourself driven to use pointers of the same nature (essentially) as Asia's enchanted boat. An army doctor who suspected you of malingering would soon reduce you to halting and contradictory statements; but if by chance you had not been malingering he would have cut himself off from all knowledge of what might have turned out an interesting case.

But are there, as I have claimed, other experiences besides sensation (and, of course, emotion) which are in this predicament? I think there are. But, frankly, I am now getting into very deep water indeed. I am almost sure I shall fail to make myself clear, but the attempt must be made.

It seems to me that imagining is something other than having mental images. When I am imagining (say, Hamlet on the battlements or Herackles' journey to the Hyperboreans) there are images in my mind. They come and go rapidly and assist what I regard as the real imagining only if I take them all as provisional make-shifts, each to be dropped as soon as it has served its (instantaneous) turn. If any one of them becomes static and grows too clear and full, imagination proper is inhibited. A too lively visual imagination is the reader's, and writer's, bane; as toys, too elaborate and realistic, spoil children's play. They are, in the etymological sense, the *offal* (the off-fall) of imagination: the slag from the furnace. Again, thinking seems to me something other than the succession of linked concepts which we use when we successfully offer our 'thought' to another in argument. That appears to me to be always a sort of translation of a prior activity: and it was the prior activity which alone enabled us to find these concepts and links. The possibility of finding them may be a good test of the value of that previous activity; certainly the only test we have. It would be dangerous to indulge ourselves with the fancy of having valuable profundities within us which (unfortunately) we can't get out. But, perhaps, in others, where we are neutrals, we are sometimes not quite wrong in thinking that a sensible man, unversed in argument, has thought better than his mis-handling of his own case suggests. If we lend him a helping hand and he replies 'Of course! That's it. That is what I really meant to say', he is not always a hypocrite. Finally, in all our joys and sorrows, religious, aesthetic, or natural, I seem to find things (almost indescribably) thus. They are *about* something. They are a by-product of the (logically) prior act of *attending to* or *looking towards* something.[1] We are not really concerned with the emotions: the emotions *are* our concern about something else. Suppose that a mother is anxious about her son who is on active service. It is no use going to her with the offer of some drug or hypnotism or spell that would obliterate her anxiety. What she wants is not the cessation of anxiety but the safety of her son (I mean, on the whole. On one particular wakeful night, she might, no doubt, be glad of your magic.) Nor is it any use offering her a magic which would prevent her from feeling any grief if her son were killed: what she dreads is not grief but the death of her son. Similarly, it is no use offering me a drug which will give me over again the feelings I had on first hearing the overture to *The Magic Flute*. The feelings, by themselves—the flutter in the

[1] *Looking towards* is neither more nor less metaphorical than *attending to*.

diaphragm—are of very mediocre interest to me. What gave them their value was the thing they were about. So in our Christian experiences. No doubt we experience sorrow when we repent and joy when we adore. But these were by-products of our attention to a particular Object.

If I have made myself at all clear (but I probably have not) you see what, for me, it adds up to. The very essence of our life as conscious beings, all day and every day, consists of something which cannot be communicated except by hints, similes, metaphors, and the use of those emotions (themselves not very important) which are pointers to it. I am not in the least talking about the Unconscious as psychologists understand it. At least, though it cannot be fully introspected, this region is, in many of us, very far from unconscious. I say 'in many of us'. But I sometimes wonder whether we may not be survivals. Evolution may not have ceased; and in evolution a species may lose old powers as well as acquire—possibly in order to acquire—new ones. There seem to be people about to whom imagination means only the presence of mental images (not to mention those like Professor Ryle who deny even that); to whom thought means only unuttered speech; and to whom emotions are final, as distinct from the things they are about. If this is so, and if they increase, then all real communications between them and the earlier type of man will finally be impossible.

Something like this may be happening. You remember Wells's *Country of the Blind.* Now its inhabitants, being men, must have descended from ancestors who could see. During centuries a gradual atrophy of sight must have spread through the whole race; but at no given moment, till it was complete, would it (probably) have been equally advanced in all individuals. During this intermediate period a very interesting linguistic situation would have arisen. They would have inherited from their unblind ancestors all the visual vocabulary—the names of the colours, words like 'see' and 'look' and 'dark' and 'light'. There would be some who still used them in the same sense as ourselves: archaic types who saw the green grass and perceived the light coming at dawn. There would be others who had faint vestiges of sight, and who used these words, with increasing vagueness, to describe sensations so evanescent as to be incapable of clear discrimination.

(The moment at which they begin to think of them as sensations in their own eyeballs, not as externals, would mark an important step.) And there would be a third class who has achieved full blindness, to whom *see* was merely a synonym for *understand* and *dark* for *difficult*. And these would be the vanguard, and the future would be with them, and a very little cross-examination of the archaic type that still saw would convince them that its attempt to give some other meaning to the old visual words was merely a tissue of vague, emotive uses and category mistakes. This would be as clear to them as it is clear to many modern people that Job's words 'But now mine eye hath seen thee: wherefore I abhor myself and repent in dust and ashes' are, and can be, nothing but the expression of an emotion.[1]

As I say, this sometimes crosses my mind. But I am full of doubts about the whole subject, and everything I have said is merely tentative. Perhaps I should also point out that it is not apologetics. I have not tried to prove that the religious sayings are true, only that they are significant: if you meet them with a certain good will, a certain readiness to find meaning. For if they should happen to contain information about real things, you will not get it on any other terms. As for proof, I sometimes wonder whether the Ontological Argument did not itself arise as a partially unsuccessful translation of an experience without concepts or words. I don't think we can initially argue from the *concept* of Perfect Being to its existence. But did they really, inside, argue from the experienced glory that it could not be generated subjectively?

[1 An interesting variation of this same theme is found in Lewis's poem, 'The Country of the Blind', *Poems*, ed. Walter Hooper, (Bles, 1964), pp. 33-34.]

PETITIONARY PRAYER:
A PROBLEM WITHOUT AN ANSWER

The problem I am submitting to you arises not about prayer in general but only about that kind of prayer which consists of request or petition. I hope no one will think that he is helping to solve my problem by reminding me that there are many other and perhaps higher sorts of prayer. I agree that there are. I here confine myself to petitionary prayer not because I think it the only, or the best, or the most characteristic, form of prayer, but because it is the form which raises the problem. However low a place we may decide to give it in the life of prayer, we must give it some place, unless we are prepared to reject both Our Lord's precept in telling us to pray for our daily bread and His practice in praying that the cup might pass from Him. And as long as it holds any place at all, I have to consider my problem.

Let me make clear at once where that problem does not lie. I am not at all concerned with the difficulty which unbelievers sometimes raise about the whole conception of petitioning God, on the ground that absolute wisdom cannot need to be informed of our desires, or that absolute goodness cannot need to be prompted to beneficence, or that the immutable and impassible cannot be affected by us, cannot be to us as patient to agent. All these difficulties are, no doubt, well worth most serious discussion, but I do not propose to discuss them here. Still less am I asking why petitions, and even the fervent petitions of holy men, are sometimes not granted. That has never seemed to me to be, in principle, a difficulty at all. That wisdom must sometimes refuse what ignorance may quite innocently ask seems to be self-evident.

My problem arises from one fact and one only; the fact that Christian teaching seems at first sight to contain two different patterns of petitionary prayer which are inconsistent: perhaps inconsistent in their theological implications, but much more obviously and pressingly inconsistent in the practical sense that no man, so far as I can see, could possibly follow them both at the same moment. I shall call them the A Pattern and the B Pattern.

The A Pattern is given in the prayer which Our Lord Himself taught us. The clause 'Thy will be done' by its very nature must modify the sense in which the following petitions are made. Under the shadow—or perhaps I should rather say, in the light—of that great submission nothing can be asked save conditionally, save in so far as the granting of it may be in accordance with God's will. I do not of course mean that the words 'Thy will be done' are merely a submission. They should, and if we make progress they will increasingly, be the voice of joyful desire, free of hunger and thirst, and I argue very heartily that to treat them simply as a clause of submission or renunciation greatly impoverishes the prayer. But though they should be something far more and better than resigned or submissive, they must not be less: they must be that *at least*. And as such they necessarily discipline all the succeeding clauses. The other specimen of the A Pattern comes from Our Lord's own example in Gethsemane. A particular event is asked for with the reservation, 'Nevertheless, not my will but thine.'

It would seem from these passages that we are directed both by Our Lord's command and by His example to make all our petitionary prayers in this conditional form; well aware that God in His wisdom may not see fit to give us what we ask and submitting our wills in advance to a possible refusal which, if it meets us, we shall know to be wholly just, merciful, and salutary. And this, I suppose, is how most of us do try to pray and how most spiritual teachers tell us to pray. With this pattern of prayer—the A Pattern—I myself would be wholly content. It is in accordance both with my heart and my head. It presents no theoretical difficulties. No doubt my rebellious will and my turbulent hopes and fears will find plenty of practical difficulty in following it. But as far as my intellect goes it is all easy. The road may be hard but the map is clear.

You will notice that in the A Pattern, whatever faith the petitioner has in the existence, the goodness, and the wisdom of God, what he obviously, even as it were by definition, has not got is a sure and unwavering belief that God will give him the particular thing he asks for. When Our Lord in Gethsemane asks that the cup may be withdrawn His words, far from implying a certainty or even a strong expectation that it will in fact be withdrawn, imply the possibility that it will not be; a possibility, or even a probability, so fully envisaged that a preparatory submission to that event is already being made.

We need not, so far as I can see, here concern ourselves with any special problems raised by the unique and holy Person of Him who prayed. It is enough to point out that if we are expected to imitate Him in our prayers, then, though we are doubtless to pray with faith in one sense, we are not to pray with any assurance that we shall receive what we ask. For real assurance that we shall receive it seems to be incompatible with the act of preparing ourselves for a denial. Men do not prepare for an event which they think impossible. And unless we think refusal impossible, how can we believe granting to be certain?

And, once again, if this were the only pattern of prayer, I should be quite content. If the faith which is demanded of us were always a faith in the goodness of God, a faith that whether granting or denying He equally gave us the best, and never a faith that He would give precisely what we ask, I should have no problem. Indeed, such a submissive faith would seem to me, if I were left to my own thoughts, far better than any confidence that our own necessarily ignorant petitions would prevail. I should be thankful that we were safe from that cruel mercy which the wiser Pagans had to dread, *numinibus vota exaudita malignis*. Even as it is I must often be glad that certain past prayers of my own were not granted.

But of course this is not the actual situation. Over against the A Pattern stands the B Pattern. Again and again in the New Testament we find the demand not for faith in such a general and (as it would seem to me) spiritual sense as I have described but for faith of a far more particular and (as it would seem to me) cruder sort: faith that the particular thing the petitioner asks will be given him. It is as if God demanded of us a faith which the Son of God in Gethsemane did not possess, and which if He had possessed it, would have been erroneous.

What springs first to mind is, of course, the long list of passages in which faith is required to those whom Our Lord healed.

Some of these may be, for our present purpose, ambiguous. Thus in Matt. ix, 22, the words 'Your faith has healed you' to the woman with the haemorrhage will be interpreted by some as a proposition not in theology but in medicine. The woman was cured by auto-suggestion: faith in any charm or quack remedy would on that view have done as well as faith in Christ—though, of course, the power in Christ to evoke faith even of that kind might have theological implications in the long run. But such a view, since it will not cover all the instances, had better not be brought in for any, on the principle of Occam's razor. And surely it can be stretched only by extreme efforts to cover instances where the faith is, so to speak, vicarious. Thus the relevant faith in the case of the sick servant (Matt. viii, 13) is not his own but that of his master the Centurion; the healing of the Canaanite child (Matt. xv, 28) depends on her mother's faith.

Again, it might perhaps be maintained that in some instances the faith in question is not a faith that this particular healing will take place but a deeper, more all-embracing faith in the Person of Christ Himself; not, of course, that the petitioners can be supposed to have believed in His deity but that they recognized and accepted His holy, or at the very least, His numinous, character. I think there is something in this view; but sometimes the faith seems to be very definitely attached to the particular gift. Thus in Matt. ix, 28, the blind men are asked not 'Do you believe in Me?' but 'Do you believe that I can do this?' Still, the words are 'that I can' not 'that I will', so we may pass that example over. But what are we to say of Matt. xiv, 31, where Peter is called ὀλιγόπιστε, because he lost his faith and sank in the waves. I should perhaps say, at this point, that I find no difficulty in accepting the walking on the water as historical. I suspect that the distinction often made between 'Nature' miracles and others seems plausible only because most of us know less about pathology and psychology than about gravitation. Perhaps if we knew all, the Divine suggestion of a single new thought to my mind would appear neither more nor less a 'Nature' miracle than stilling the storm or feeding the five thousand. But that is not a point I wish to raise. I am concerned only with the implications of ὀλιγόπιστε. For it would seem that St Peter might have had any degree of faith in the goodness and power of God and even in the Deity of Christ and yet been wholly uncertain whether he could continue walking on the water For in that case his faith would surely have told him that whether he walked or whether he sank he was equally in God's hands, and, submitting himself in the spirit of the Gethsemane prayer, he would have prepared himself, so far as infirmity allowed, to glorify God either by living or by drowning, and his failure, if he failed, would have been due to an imperfect mortification of instinct but not to a lack (in that sense) of faith. The faith which he is accused of lacking must surely be faith in the particular event: the continued walking on water.

All these examples, however, might be dismissed on the ground that they are not, in one strict sense of the word, examples of prayer. Let us then turn to those that are.

Whether you will agree to include Matt. xxi, 21, I don't know. Our Lord there says ἐὰν ἔχητε πίστιν καὶ μὴ διακριθῆτε, 'If you have faith with no hesitations or reservations, you can tell a mountain to throw itself into the sea and it will.' I very much hope that no one will solemnly remind us that Our Lord, according to the flesh, was an Oriental and that Orientals use hyperboles, and think that this has disposed of the passage. Of course Orientals, and Occidentals, use hyperboles, and of course Our Lord's first hearers did not suppose Him to mean that large and highly mischievous disturbances of the landscape would be common or edifying operations of faith. But a sane man does not use hyperbole to mean nothing: by a great thing (which is not literally true) he suggests a great thing which is. When he says that someone's heart is broken he does not mean that this organ is literally fractured, but he does mean that the person in question is in very great anguish. Only a windbag says 'His heart is broken' when he means 'He is somewhat depressed.' And if all Orientals were doomed by the mere fact of being Orientals to be windbags (which of course they are not) the Truth Himself, the Wisdom of the Father, would not and could not have been united with the human nature of an Oriental. (The point is worth making. Some people make allowances for local and temporary conditions in the speeches of Our Lord on a scale which really implies that God chose the time and place of the Incarnation very injudiciously.) Our Lord need not mean the words about the mountain literally; but at the very least they must mean doing some mighty work. The point is that the condition of doing such a mighty work is unwavering, unhesitating faith. Indeed He goes on in the very next sentence to make the same statement without any figures of speech at all: πάντα ὅσα ἂν αἰτήσητε ἐν τῇ προσευχῇ πιστεύοντες λήψεσθε.[1]

Can we even here take πιστεύοντες to mean 'having a general faith in the power and goodness of God'? We cannot. The corresponding passage in Mark,[2] though it adds a new difficulty, makes this point at least embarrassingly plain. The words are πάντα ὅσα προσεύχεσθε καὶ αἰτεῖσθε πιστεύετε ὅτι ἐλάβετε καὶ ἔσται ὑμῖν. The tense, present or (worse still) aorist, is of course perplexing. I hope someone will explain to us what either might represent in Aramaic. But there is no doubt at all that what we are to believe is precisely that we get 'all the things' we ask for. We are not to believe that we shall get either what we ask or else something far better: we are to believe that we shall get those very things. It is a faith, unwavering faith in that event, to which success is promised.

The same astonishing—and even, to my natural feelings, shocking—promise is repeated elsewhere with additions which may or may not turn out to be helpful for our present purpose.

In Matt. xviii, 19, we learn that if two (or two or three) agree in a petition it will be granted. Faith is not explicitly mentioned here but is no doubt assumed: if it were not, the promise would be only the more startling and the further (I think) from the pattern of Gethsemane. The reason for the promise follows: 'For where two or three are gathered together εἰς τὸ ἐμὸν ὄνομα, there am I in their midst.' With this goes John xiv, 13, 'Whatever you ask in my name, I will do this': not this or something far better, but 'whatever you ask'.

I have discovered that some people find in these passages a solution of the whole problem. For here we have the prayer of the Church (as soon as two or three are gathered together in that

---

[1 Matt. xxi, 22: 'And whatever you ask in prayer, you will receive, if you have faith.']

[2 Mark xi, 23–4: 'Truly, I say to you, whoever says to this mountain, "Be taken up and cast into the sea", and does not doubt in his heart, but believes that what he says will come to pass, it will be done for him. Therefore I tell you, whatever you ask in prayer, believe that you receive it, and you will."']

Name) and the presence of Christ in the Church: so that the prayer which is granted by the Father is the prayer of the Son, and prayer and answer alike are an operation within the Deity.

I agree that this makes the promises less startling; but does it reconcile them with the A Pattern? And does it reconcile them with the facts? For surely there have been occasions on which the whole Church prays and is refused? I suppose that at least twice in this century the whole Church prayed for peace and no peace was given her. I think, however we define the Church, we must say that the whole Church prayed: peasants in Italy and popes in Russian villages, elders at Peebles, Anglicans in Cambridge, Congregationalists in Liverpool, Salvationists in East London. You may say (though I would not) that some who prayed were not in the Church; but it would be hard to find any in the Church who did not pray. But the cup did not pass from them. I am not, in principle, puzzled by the fact of the refusal: what I am puzzled by is the promise of granting.

And this at once raises a question which shows how frighteningly practical the problem is. *How* did the Church pray? Did she use the A Pattern or the B? Did she pray with unwavering confidence that peace would be given, or did she humbly follow the example of Gethsemane, adding 'If it be Thy will . . . not as I will, but as Thou wilt', preparing herself in advance for a refusal of that particular blessing and putting all her faith into the belief that even if it were denied, the denial would be full of mercy? I am disposed to believe that she did the latter. And was that, conceivably, her ghastly mistake? Was she like the διακρινόμενος, the man of doubtful faith who, as St James tells us,[1] must not suppose that he will receive anything? Have all my own intercessory prayers for years been mistaken? For I have always prayed that the illnesses of my friends might be healed 'if it was God's will', very clearly envisaging the possibility that it might not be. Perhaps this has all been a fake humility and a false spirituality for which my friends owe me little thanks; perhaps I ought never to have dreamed of refusal, μηδὲν διακρινόμενος?

[1 James i, 6–8: 'But let him ask in faith, with no doubting, for he who doubts is like a wave of the sea that is driven and tossed by the wind. For that person must not suppose that a double-minded man, unstable in all his ways, will receive anything from the Lord.']

148

Again, if the true prayer is joined with the prayer of the Church and hers with the prayer of Christ, and is therefore irresistible, was not it Christ who prayed in Gethsemane, using a different method and meeting with denial?

Another attempted solution runs something like this. The promise is made to prayers in Christ's name. And this of course means not simply prayers which end with the formula 'Through Jesus Christ Our Lord' but prayers prayed in the spirit of Christ, prayers uttered by us when, and in so far as, we are 'in' Him. Such prayers are the ones that can be made with unwavering faith that the blessing we ask for will be given us. And this may be supported (though I suspect it had better not be) from I John v, 14, 'Whatever we ask Him according to His will, He will hear us.' But how are we to hold this view and yet avoid the implication (*quod nefas dicere*) that Christ Himself in Gethsemane failed to pray in the spirit of Christ, since He neither used the form which that spirit is held to justify nor received the answer which that spirit is held to insure? As for the Johannine passage, would we dare to produce it in this context before an audience of intelligent but simple inquirers. They come to us (this often happens) saying that they have been told that those who pray in faith to the Christian God will get what they ask: that they have tried it and not got what they asked: and what, please, is our explanation? Dare we say that when God promises 'You shall have what you ask' He secretly means 'You shall have it if you ask for something I wish to give you'? What should we think of an earthly father who promised to give his son whatever he chose for his birthday and, when the boy asked for a bicycle gave him an arithmetic book, then first disclosing the silent reservation with which the promise was made?

Of course the arithmetic book may be better for the son than the bicycle, and a robust faith may manage to believe so. That is not where the difficulty, the sense of cruel mockery, lies. The boy is tempted, not to complain that the bicycle was denied, but that the promise of 'anything he chose' was made. So with us.

It is possible that someone present may be wholly on the side of the B Pattern: someone who has seen many healed by prayer. Such a person will be tempted to reply that most of us are in fact grievously wrong in our prayer-life: that miracles are accorded to unwavering faith: that if we dropped our disobedient lowliness and pseudo-spiritual timidity blessings we never dreamed of would be showered on us at every turn. I certainly would not hear such a person with scepticism, still less with mockery. I believe in miracles, here and now. But if this is the complete answer, then why was the A Pattern of prayer ever given at all?

I have no answer to my problem, though I have taken it to about every Christian I know, learned or simple, lay or clerical, within my own Communion or without. Before closing I have, however, one hesitant observation to make.

One thing seems to be clear to me. Whatever else faith may mean (that is, faith in the granting of the blessing asked, for with faith in any other sense we need not at this point be concerned) I feel quite sure that it does not mean any state of psychological certitude such as might be—I think it sometimes is—manufactured from within by the natural action of a strong will upon an obedient imagination. The faith that moves mountains is a gift from Him who created mountains. That being so, can I ease my problem by saying that until God gives me such a faith I have no practical decision to make; I must pray after the A Pattern because, in fact, I cannot pray after the B Pattern? If, on the other hand, God even gave me such a faith, then again I should have no decision to make; I should find myself praying in the B Pattern. This would fall in with an old opinion of my own that we ought all of us to be ashamed of not performing miracles and that we do not feel this shame enough. We regard our own state as normal and theurgy as exceptional, whereas we ought perhaps to regard the worker of miracles, however rare, as the true Christian norm and ourselves as spiritual cripples. Yet I do not find this quite a satisfactory solution. I think we might get over the prayer in Gethsemane. We might say that in His tender humility Our Lord, just as He refused the narcotic wine mingled with myrrh, and just as He chose (I think) to be united to a human nature not of iron nerves but to a nature sensitive, shrinking, and unable not to live through torture in advance, so He chose on that night to plumb the depths of Christian experience, to resemble not the heroes of His army but the very weakest camp followers and unfits; or even that such a choice is implied in those unconsciously profound and involuntarily blessed words 'He saved others, Himself He cannot save.' But some discomfort remains. I do not like to represent God as saying 'I will grant what you ask in faith' and adding, so to speak, 'Because I will not give you the faith—not that kind—unless you ask what I want to give you.' Once more, there is just a faint suggestion of mockery, of goods that look a little larger in the advertisement than they turn out to be. Not that we complain of any defect in the goods: it is the faintest suspicion of excess in the advertisement that is disquieting. But at present I have got no further. I come to you, reverend Fathers, for guidance. How am I to pray this very night?

MODERN THEOLOGY AND BIBLICAL
CRITICISM

This paper arose out of a conversation I had with the Principal[1]
one night last term. A book of Alec Vidler's happened to be lying
on the table and I expressed my reaction to the sort of theology
it contained. My reaction was a hasty and ignorant one, produced
with the freedom that comes after dinner.[2] One thing led to
another and before we were done I was saying a good deal more
than I had meant about the type of thought which, so far as I
could gather, is now dominant in many theological colleges. He
then said, 'I wish you would come and say all this to my young
men.' He knew of course that I was extremely ignorant of the
whole thing. But I think his idea was that you ought to know how
a certain sort of theology strikes the outsider. Though I may have
nothing but misunderstandings to lay before you, you ought to
know that such misunderstandings exist. That sort of thing is easy
to overlook inside one's own circle. The minds you daily meet
have been conditioned by the same studies and prevalent opinions
as your own. That may mislead you. For of course as priests it is
the outsiders you will have to cope with. You exist in the long
run for no other purpose. The proper study of shepherds is sheep,
not (save accidentally) other shepherds. And woe to you if you
do not evangelize. I am not trying to teach my grandmother. I am
a sheep, telling shepherds what only a sheep can tell them. And
now I start my bleating.

There are two sorts of outsiders: the uneducated, and those

[1 The Principal of Westcott House, Cambridge, now the Bishop of Edin-
burgh (The Rt Rev Kenneth Carey).]

[2 While the Bishop was out of the room, Lewis read 'The Sign at Cana' in
Alec Vidler's Windsor Sermons (S.C.M. Press, 1958). The Bishop recalls that
when he asked him what he thought about it, Lewis 'expressed himself very
freely about the sermon and said that he thought that it was quite incredible
that we should have had to wait nearly 2,000 years to be told by a theologian
called Vidler that what the Church has always regarded as a miracle was, in fact,
a parable!']

who are educated in some way but not in your way. How you are to deal with the first class, if you hold views like Loisy's or Schweitzer's or Bultmann's or Tillich's or even Alec Vidler's, I simply don't know. I see—and I'm told that you see—that it would hardly do to tell them what you really believe. A theology which denies the historicity of nearly everything in the Gospels to which Christian life and affections and thought have been fastened for nearly two millennia—which either denies the miraculous altogether or, more strangely, after swallowing the camel of the Resurrection strains at such gnats as the feeding of the multitudes—if offered to the uneducated man can produce only one or other of two effects. It will make him a Roman Catholic or an atheist. What you offer him he will not recognize as Christianity. If he holds to what he calls Christianity he will leave a Church in which it is no longer taught and look for one where it is. If he agrees with your version he will no longer call himself a Christian and no longer come to church. In his crude, coarse way, he would respect you much more if you did the same. An experienced clergyman told me that most liberal priests, faced with this problem, have recalled from its grave the late medieval conception of two truths: a picture-truth which can be preached to the people, and an esoteric truth for use among the clergy. I shouldn't think you will enjoy this conception much when you have to put it into practice. I'm sure if I had to produce picture-truths to a parishioner in great anguish or under fierce temptation, and produce them with that seriousness and fervour which his condition demanded, while knowing all the time that I didn't exactly—only in some Pickwickian sense—believe them myself, I'd find my forehead getting red and damp and my collar getting tight. But that is your headache, not mine. You have, after all, a different sort of collar. I claim to belong to the second group of outsiders: educated, but not theologically educated. How one member of that group feels I must now try to tell you.

The undermining of the old orthodoxy has been mainly the work of divines engaged in New Testament criticism. The authority of experts in that discipline is the authority in deference to whom we are asked to give up a huge mass of beliefs shared in common by the early Church, the Fathers, the Middle Ages, the Reformers, and even the nineteenth century. I want to explain what it is that makes me sceptical about this authority. Ignorantly sceptical, as you will all too easily see. But the scepticism is the father of the ignorance. It is hard to persevere in a close study when you can work up no *prima facie* confidence in your teachers.

First then, whatever these men may be as Biblical critics, I distrust them as critics. They seem to me to lack literary judgement, to be imperceptive about the very quality of the texts they are reading. It sounds a strange charge to bring against men who have been steeped in those books all their lives. But that might be just the trouble. A man who has spent his youth and manhood in the minute study of New Testament texts and of other people's studies of them, whose literary experiences of those texts lacks any standard of comparison such as can only grow from a wide and deep and genial experience of literature in general, is, I should think, very likely to miss the obvious things about them. If he tells me that something in a Gospel is legend or romance, I want to know how many legends and romances he has read, how well his palate is trained in detecting them by the flavour; not how many years he has spent on that Gospel. But I had better turn to examples.

In what is already a very old commentary I read that the Fourth Gospel is regarded by one school as a 'spiritual romance', 'a poem not a history', to be judged by the same canons as Nathan's parable, the Book of Jonah, *Paradise Lost* 'or, more exactly, *Pilgrim's Progress*'.[1] After a man has said that, why need one attend to anything else he says about any book in the world? Note that he regards *Pilgrim's Progress*, a story which professes to be a dream and flaunts its allegorical nature by every single proper name it uses, as the closest parallel. Note that the whole epic panoply of Milton goes for nothing. But even if we leave out the grosser absurdities and keep to *Jonah*, the insensitiveness is crass—*Jonah*, a tale with as few even pretended historical attachments as *Job*, grotesque in incident and surely not without a distinct, though of

[1 Lewis is quoting from an article, 'The Gospel According to St. John', by Walter Lock in *A New Commentary on Holy Scripture, including the Apocrypha*, ed. by Charles Gore, Henry Leighton Goudge, Alfred Guillaume (S.P.C.K., 1928), p. 241. Lock, in turn, is quoting from James Drummond's *An Inquiry into the Character and Authorship of the Fourth Gospel* (Williams and Norgate, 1903).]

course edifying, vein of typically Jewish humour. Then turn to John. Read the dialogues: that with the Samaritan woman at the well, or that which follows the healing of the man born blind. Look at its pictures: Jesus (if I may use the word) doodling with his finger in the dust; the unforgettable ἦν δὲ νύξ (xiii, 30). I have been reading poems, romances, vision-literature, legends, myths all my life. I know what they are like. I know that not one of them is like this. Of this text there are only two possible views. Either this is reportage—though it may no doubt contain errors—pretty close up to the facts; nearly as close as Boswell. Or else, some unknown writer in the second century, without known predecessors or successors, suddenly anticipated the whole technique of modern, novelistic, realistic narrative. If it is untrue, it must be narrative of that kind. The reader who doesn't see this has simply not learned to read. I would recommend him to read Auerbach.[1]

Here, from Bultmann's *Theology of the New Testament* (p. 30) is another: 'Observe in what unassimilated fashion the prediction of the parousia (Mk. viii, 38) follows upon the prediction of the passion (viii, 31).'[2] What can he mean? Unassimilated? Bultmann believes that predictions of the parousia are older than those of the passion. He therefore wants to believe—and no doubt does believe —that when they occur in the same passage some discrepancy or 'unassimilation' must be perceptible between them. But surely he foists this on the text with shocking lack of perception. Peter has confessed Jesus to be the Anointed One. That flash of glory is hardly over before the dark prophecy begins—that the Son of Man must suffer and die. Then this contrast is repeated. Peter, raised for a moment by his confession, makes his false step; the crushing rebuff 'Get thee behind me' follows. Then, across that momentary ruin which Peter (as so often) becomes, the voice of the Master, turning to the crowd, generalizes the moral. All His followers must take up the cross. This avoidance of suffering, this self-preservation, is not what life is really about. Then, more definitely still, the summons to martyrdom. You must stand to your tackling. If you disown Christ here and now, He will disown

[1 Lewis means, I think, Erich Auerbach's *Mimesis: The Representation of Reality in Western Literature*, translated by Williard R. Trask (Princeton, 1953).]

[2 Rudolf Bultmann, *Theology of the New Testament*, translated by Kendrick Grobel, vol. I (S.C.M. Press, 1952), p. 30.]

you later. Logically, emotionally, imaginatively, the sequence is perfect. Only a Bultmann could think otherwise.

Finally, from the same Bultmann: 'The personality of Jesus has no importance for the kerygma either of Paul or of John ... Indeed the tradition of the earliest Church did not even unconsciously preserve a picture of his personality. Every attempt to reconstruct one remains a play of subjective imagination.'[1]

So there is no personality of Our Lord presented in the New Testament. Through what strange process has this learned German gone in order to make himself blind to what all men except him see? What evidence have we that he would recognize a personality if it were there? For it is Bultmann *contra mundum*. If anything whatever is common to all believers, and even to many unbelievers, it is the sense that in the Gospels they have met a personality. There are characters whom we know to be historical but of whom we do not feel that we have any personal knowledge—knowledge by acquaintance; such are Alexander, Attila, or William of Orange. There are others who make no claim to historical reality but whom, none the less, we know as we know real people: Falstaff, Uncle Toby, Mr Pickwick. But there are only three characters who, claiming the first sort of reality, also actually have the second. And surely everyone knows who they are: Plato's Socrates, the Jesus of the Gospels, and Boswell's Johnson. Our acquaintance with them shows itself in a dozen ways. When we look into the Apocryphal gospels, we find ourselves constantly saying of this or that *logion*, 'No. It's a fine saying, but not His. That wasn't how He talked.'—just as we do with all pseudo-Johnsoniana. We are not in the least perturbed by the contrasts within each character: the union in Socrates of silly and scabrous titters about Greek pederasty with the highest mystical fervour and the homeliest good sense; in Johnson, of profound gravity and melancholy with that love of fun and nonsense which Boswell never understood though Fanny Burney did; in Jesus of peasant shrewdness, intolerable severity, and irresistible tenderness. So strong is the flavour of the personality that, even while He says things which, on any other assumption than that of Divine Incarnation in the fullest sense, would be appallingly arrogant, yet we—and many unbelievers too—accept Him at His own

[1 *Op. cit.*, p. 35.]

valuation when He says 'I am meek and lowly of heart.' Even those passages in the New Testament which superficially, and in intention, are most concerned with the Divine, and least with the Human Nature, bring us face to face with the personality. I am not sure that they don't do this more than any others. 'We beheld His glory, the glory as of the only begotten of the Father, full of graciousness and reality . . . which we have looked upon and our hands have handled.' What is gained by trying to evade or dissipate this shattering immediacy of personal contact by talk about 'that significance which the early church found that it was impelled to attribute to the Master'? This hits us in the face. Not what they were impelled to do but what impelled them. I begin to fear that by *personality* Dr Bultmann means what I should call impersonality: what you'd get in a D.N.B. article or an obituary or a Victorian *Life and Letters of Yeshua Bar-Yosef* in three volumes with photographs.

That then is my first bleat. These men ask me to believe they can read between the lines of the old texts; the evidence is their obvious inability to read (in any sense worth discussing) the lines themselves. They claim to see fern-seed and can't see an elephant ten yards away in broad daylight.

Now for my second bleat. All theology of the liberal type involves at some point—and often involves throughout—the claim that the real behaviour and purpose and teaching of Christ came very rapidly to be misunderstood and misrepresented by His followers, and has been recovered or exhumed only by modern scholars. Now long before I became interested in theology I had met this kind of theory elsewhere. The tradition of Jowett still dominated the study of ancient philosophy when I was reading Greats. One was brought up to believe that the real meaning of Plato had been misunderstood by Aristotle and wildly travestied by the neo-Platonists, only to be recovered by the moderns. When recovered, it turned out (most fortunately) that Plato had really all along been an English Hegelian, rather like T. H. Green. I have met it a third time in my own professional studies; every week a clever undergraduate, every quarter a dull American don, discovers for the first time what some Shakesperian play really meant. But in this third instance I am a privileged person. The revolution in thought and sentiment which has occurred in my own lifetime is so great that I belong, mentally, to Shakespeare's world far more than to that of these recent interpreters. I see—I feel it in my bones—I know beyond argument—that most of their interpretations are merely impossible; they involve a way of looking at things which was not known in 1914, much less in the Jacobean period. This daily confirms my suspicion of the same approach to Plato or the New Testament. The idea that any man or writer should be opaque to those who lived in the same culture, spoke the same language, shared the same habitual imagery and unconscious assumptions, and yet be transparent to those who have none of these advantages, is in my opinion preposterous. There is an *a priori* improbability in it which almost no argument and no evidence could counterbalance.

Thirdly, I find in these theologians a constant use of the principle that the miraculous does not occur. Thus any statement put into Our Lord's mouth by the old texts, which, if He had really made it, would constitute a prediction of the future, is taken to have been put in after the occurrence which it seemed to predict. This is very sensible if we start by knowing that inspired prediction can never occur. Similarly in general, the rejection as unhistorical of all passages which narrate miracles is sensible if we start by knowing that the miraculous in general never occurs. Now I do not here want to discuss whether the miraculous is possible. I only want to point out that this is a purely philosophical question. Scholars, as scholars, speak on it with no more authority than anyone else. The canon 'If miraculous, unhistorical' is one they bring to their study of the texts, not one they have learned from it. If one is speaking of authority, the united authority of all the Biblical critics in the world counts here for nothing. On this they speak simply as men; men obviously influenced by, and perhaps insufficiently critical of, the spirit of the age they grew up in.

But my fourth bleat—which is also my loudest and longest—is still to come.

All this sort of criticism attempts to reconstruct the genesis of the texts it studies; what vanished documents each author used, when and where he wrote, with what purposes, under what influences—the whole *Sitz im Leben* of the text. This is done with immense erudition and great ingenuity. And at first sight it is very convincing. I think I should be convinced by it myself, but that I carry about with me a charm—the herb *moly*—against it. You must excuse me if I now speak for a while of myself. The value of what I say depends on its being first-hand evidence.

What forearms me against all these Reconstructions is the fact that I have seen it all from the other end of the stick. I have watched reviewers reconstructing the genesis of my own books in just this way.

Until you come to be reviewed yourself you would never believe how little of an ordinary review is taken up by criticism in the strict sense: by evaluation, praise, or censure, of the book actually written. Most of it is taken up with imaginary histories of the process by which you wrote it. The very terms which the reviewers use in praising or dispraising often imply such a history. They praise a passage as 'spontaneous' and censure another as 'laboured'; that is, they think they know that you wrote the one *currente calamo* and the other *invita Minerva*.

What the value of such reconstructions is I learned very early in my career. I had published a book of essays; and the one into which I had put most of my heart, the one I really cared about and in which I discharged a keen enthusiasm, was on William Morris.[1] And in almost the first review I was told that this was obviously the only one in the book in which I had felt no interest. Now don't mistake. The critic was, I now believe, quite right in thinking it the worst essay in the book; at least everyone agreed with him. Where he was totally wrong was in his imaginary history of the causes which produced its dullness.

Well, this made me prick up my ears. Since then I have watched with some care similar imaginary histories both of my own books and of books by friends whose real history I knew. Reviewers, both friendly and hostile, will dash you off such histories with great confidence; will tell you what public events had directed the author's mind to this or that, what other authors had influenced him, what his over-all intention was, what sort of audience he principally addressed, why—and when—he did everything.

Now I must first record my impression; then, distinct from it, what I can say with certainty. My impression is that in the whole

[1 Lewis's essay on 'William Morris' appears in *Rehabilitations and Other Essays* (Oxford, 1939).]

159

of my experience not one of these guesses has on any one point been right; that the method shows a record of 100 per cent. failure. You would expect that by mere chance they would hit as often as they miss. But it is my impression that they do no such thing. I can't remember a single hit. But as I have not kept a careful record my mere impression may be mistaken. What I think I can say with certainty is that they are usually wrong.

And yet they would often sound—if you didn't know the truth —extremely convincing. Many reviewers said that the Ring in Tolkien's *The Lord of the Rings* was suggested by the atom bomb. What could be more plausible? Here is a book published when everyone was preoccupied by that sinister invention; here in the centre of the book is a weapon which it seems madness to throw away yet fatal to use. Yet in fact, the chronology of the book's composition makes the theory impossible. Only the other week a reviewer said that a fairy tale by my friend Roger Lancelyn Green was influenced by fairy tales of mine. Nothing could be more probable. I have an imaginary country with a beneficent lion in it: Green, one with a beneficent tiger. Green and I can be proved to read one another's works; to be indeed in various ways closely associated. The case for an affiliation is far stronger than many which we accept as conclusive when dead authors are concerned. But it's all untrue nevertheless. I know the genesis of that Tiger and that Lion and they are quite independent.[1]

Now this surely ought to give us pause. The reconstruction of the history of a text, when the text is ancient, sounds very convincing. But one is after all sailing by dead reckoning; the results cannot be checked by fact. In order to decide how reliable the method is, what more could you ask for than to be shown an

[1 Lewis corrected this error in the following letter, 'Books for Children', in *The Times Literary Supplement* (28 November 1958), p. 689: 'Sir,—A review of Mr R. L. Green's *Land of the Lord High Tiger* in your issue of 21 November spoke of myself (in passing) with so much kindness that I am reluctant to cavil at anything it contained: but in justice to Mr Green I must. The critic suggested that Mr Green's Tiger owed something to my fairy-tales. In reality this is not so and is chronologically impossible. The Tiger was an old inhabitant, and his land a familiar haunt, of Mr Green's imagination long before I began writing. There is a moral here for all of us as critics. I wonder how much *Quellenforschung* in our studies of older literature seems solid only because those who knew the facts are dead and cannot contradict it?']

instance where the same method is at work and we have facts to check it by? Well, that is what I have done. And we find, that when this check is available, the results are either always, or else nearly always, wrong. The 'assured results of modern scholarship', as to the way in which an old book was written, are 'assured', we may conclude, only because the men who knew the facts are dead and can't blow the gaff. The huge essays in my own field which reconstruct the history of *Piers Plowman* or *The Faerie Queene* are most unlikely to be anything but sheer illusions.[1]

Am I then venturing to compare every whipster who writes a review in a modern weekly with these great scholars who have devoted their whole lives to the detailed study of the New Testament? If the former are always wrong, does it follow that the latter must fare no better?

There are two answers to this, First, while I respect the learning of the great Biblical critics, I am not yet persuaded that their judgement is equally to be respected. But, secondly, consider with what overwhelming advantages the mere reviewers start. They reconstruct the history of a book written by someone whose mother-tongue is the same as theirs; a contemporary, educated like themselves, living in something like the same mental and spiritual climate. They have everything to help them. The superiority in judgement and diligence which you are going to attribute to the Biblical critics will have to be almost superhuman if it is to offset the fact that they are everywhere faced with customs, language, race-characteristics, class-characteristics, a religious background, habits of composition, and basic assumptions, which no scholarhsip will ever enable any man now alive to know as surely and intimately and instinctively as the reviewer can know mine. And for the very same reason, remember, the Biblical critics, whatever reconstructions they devise, can never be crudely proved wrong. St Mark is dead. When they meet St Peter there will be more pressing matters to discuss.

You may say, of course, that such reviewers are foolish in so far as they guess how a sort of book they never wrote themselves was written by another. They assume that you wrote a story as

[1 For a fuller treatment on book-reviewing, see Lewis's essay 'On Criticism' in his *Of Other Worlds: Essays and Stories*, ed. Walter Hooper, (Bles, 1966), pp. 43–58.]

they would try to write a story; the fact that they would so try, explains why they have not produced any stories. But are the Biblical critics in this way much better off? Dr Bultmann never wrote a gospel. Has the experience of his learned, specialized, and no doubt meritorious, life really given him any power of seeing into the minds of those long dead men who were caught up into what, on any view, must be regarded as the central religious experience of the whole human race? It is no incivility to say—he himself would admit—that he must in every way be divided from the evangelists by far more formidable barriers—spiritual as well as intellectual—than any that could exist between my reviewers and me.

My picture of one layman's reaction—and I think it is not a rare one—would be incomplete without some account of the hopes he secretly cherishes and the naïve reflections with which he sometimes keeps his spirits up.

You must face the fact he does not expect the present school of theological thought to be everlasting. He thinks, perhaps wishfully thinks, that the whole thing may blow over. I have learned in other fields of study how transitory the 'assured results of modern scholarship' may be, how soon scholarship ceases to be modern. The confident treatment to which the New Testament is subjected is no longer applied to profane texts. There used to be English scholars who were prepared to cut up *Henry VI* between half a dozen authors and assign his share to each. We don't do that now. When I was a boy one would have been laughed at for supposing there had been a real Homer: the disintegrators seemed to have triumphed forever. But Homer seems to be creeping back. Even the belief of the ancient Greeks that the Mycenaeans were their ancestors and spoke Greek has been surprisingly supported. We may without disgrace believe in a historical Arthur. Everywhere, except in theology, there has been a vigorous growth of scepticism about scepticism itself. We can't keep ourselves from murmuring *multa renascentur quae jam cecidere*.

Nor can a man of my age ever forget how suddenly and completely the idealist philosophy of his youth fell. McTaggart, Green, Bosanquet, Bradley seemed enthroned forever; they went down as suddenly as the Bastille. And the interesting thing is that while I lived under that dynasty I felt various difficulties and objections which I never dared to express. They were so fright-fully obvious that I felt sure they must be mere misunderstandings: the great men could not have made such very elementary mis-takes as those which my objections implied. But very similar objections—though put, no doubt, far more cogently than I could have put them—were among the criticisms which finally prevailed. They would now be the stock answers to English Hegeli-anism. If anyone present tonight has felt the same shy and tenta-tive doubts about the great Biblical critics, perhaps he need not feel quite certain that they are only his stupidity. They may have a future he little dreams of.

We derive a little comfort, too, from our mathematical col-leagues. When a critic reconstructs the genesis of a text he usually has to use what may be called linked hypotheses. Thus Bultmann says that Peter's confession is 'an Easter-story projected backward into Jesus' life-time' (p. 26, *op. cit.*). The first hypothesis is that Peter made no such confession. Then, granting that, there is a second hypothesis as to how the false story of his having done so might have grown up. Now let us suppose—what I am far from granting—that the first hypothesis has a probability of 90 per cent. Let us assume that the second hypothesis also has a proba-bility of 90 per cent. But the two together don't still have 90 per cent·, for the second comes in only on the assumption of the first. You have not A plus B; you have a complex AB. And the mathe-maticians tell me that AB has only an 81 per cent. probability. I'm not good enough at arithmetic to work it out, but you see that if, in a complex reconstruction, you go on thus superin-ducing hypothesis on hypothesis, you will in the end get a com-plex in which, though each hypothesis by itself has in a sense a high probability, the whole has almost none.

You must not, however, paint the picture too black. We are not fundamentalists. We think that different elements in this sort of theology have different degrees of strength. The nearer it sticks to mere textual criticism, of the old sort, Lachmann's sort, the more we are disposed to believe in it. And of course we agree that passages almost verbally identical cannot be independent. It is as we glide away from this into reconstructions of a subtler and more ambitious kind that our faith in the method wavers; and our faith in Christianity is proportionately corroborated. The sort of statement that arouses our deepest scepticism is the statement that something in a Gospel cannot be historical because it shows a theology or an ecclesiology too developed for so early a date. For this implies that we know, first of all, that there was any development in the matter, and secondly, how quickly it proceeded. It even implies an extraordinary homogeneity and continuity of development: implicitly denies that anyone could greatly have anticipated anyone else. This seems to involve knowing about a number of long dead people—for the early Christians were, after all, people—things of which I believe few of us could have given an accurate account if we had lived among them; all the forward and backward surge of discussion, preaching, and individual religious experience. I could not speak with similar confidence about the circle I have chiefly lived in myself. I could not describe the history even of my own thought as confidently as these men describe the history of the early Church's mind. And I am perfectly certain no one else could. Suppose a future scholar knew that I abandoned Christianity in my teens, and that, also in my teens, I went to an atheist tutor. Would not this seem far better evidence than most of what we have about the development of Christian theology in the first two centuries? Would he not conclude that my apostasy was due to the tutor? And then reject as 'backward projection' any story which represented me as an atheist before I went to that tutor? Yet he would be wrong. I am sorry to have become once more autobiographical. But reflection on the extreme improbability of his own life—by historical standards—seems to me a profitable exercise for everyone. It encourages a due agnosticism.

For agnosticism is, in a sense, what I am preaching. I do not wish to reduce the sceptical element in your minds. I am only suggesting that it need not be reserved exclusively for the New Testament and the Creeds. Try doubting something else.

Such scepticism might, I think, begin at the very beginning with the thought which underlies the whole demythology of our time. It was put long ago by Tyrrell. As man progresses he revolts against 'earlier and inadequate expressions of the religious idea ... Taken literally, and not symbolically, they do not meet his need. And as long as he demands to picture to himself distinctly the term and satisfaction of that need he is doomed to doubt, for his picturings will necessarily be drawn from the world of his present experience.'[1]

In one way of course Tyrrell was saying nothing new. The Negative Theology of Pseudo-Dionysius had said as much, but it drew no such conclusions as Tyrrell. Perhaps this is because the older tradition found our conceptions inadequate to God whereas Tyrrell finds it inadequate to 'the religious idea'. He doesn't say whose idea. But I am afraid he means Man's idea. We, being men, know what we think: and we find the doctrines of the Resurrection, the Ascension, and the Second Coming inadequate to our thoughts. But supposing these things were the expressions of God's thought?

It might still be true that 'taken literally and not symbolically' they are inadequate. From which the conclusion commonly drawn is that they must be taken symbolically, not literally; that is, wholly symbolically. All the details are equally symbolical and analogical.

But surely there is a flaw here. The argument runs like this. All the details are derived from our present experience; but the reality transcends our experience: therefore all the details are wholly and equally symbolical. But suppose a dog were trying to form a conception of human life. All the details in its picture would be derived from canine experience. Therefore all that the dog imagined could, at best, be only analogically true of human life. The conclusion is false. If the dog visualized our scientific researches in terms of ratting, this would be analogical; but if it thought that eating could be predicated of humans only in an analogical sense, the dog would be wrong. In fact if a dog could, *per impossibile*, be plunged for a day into human life, it would be hardly more surprised by hitherto unimagined differences than by hitherto unsuspected similarities. A reverent dog would be shocked. A modernist dog, distrusting the whole experience, would ask to be taken to the vet.

But the dog can't get into human life. Consequently, though it can be sure that its best ideas of human life are full af analogy and symbol, it could never point to any one detail and say, 'This is entirely symbolic.' You cannot know that everything in the

[1 George Tyrrell, 'The Apocalyptic Vision of Christ' in *Christianity at the Cross-Roads* (Longmans, Green & Co., 1909), p. 125.]

representation of a thing is symbolical unless you have independent access to the thing and can compare it with the representation. Dr Tyrrell can tell that the story of the Ascension is
inadequate to his religious idea, because he knows his own idea
and can compare it with the story. But how if we are asking
about a transcendent, objective reality to which the story is our
sole access? 'We know not—oh we know not.' But then we must
take our ignorance seriously.

Of course if 'taken literally and not symbolically' means 'taken
in terms of mere physics', then this story is not even a religious
story. Motion away from the earth—which is what Ascension
physically means—would not in itself be an event of spiritual
significance. Therefore, you argue, the spiritual reality can have
nothing but an analogical connection with the story of an ascent.
For the union of God with God and of Man with God-man can
have nothing to do with space. Who told you this? What you
really mean is that we can't see how it could possibly have anything to do with it. That is a quite different proposition. When I
know as I am known I shall be able to tell which parts of the story
were purely symbolical and which, if any, were not; shall see how
the transcendent reality either excludes and repels locality, or how
unimaginably it assimilates and loads it with significance. Had
we not better wait?

Such are the reactions of one bleating layman to Modern
Theology. It is right you should hear them. You will not perhaps
hear them very often again. Your parishioners will not often
speak to you quite frankly. Once the layman was anxious to hide
the fact that he believed so much less than the Vicar: he now tends
to hide the fact that he believes so much more. Missionary to the
priests of one's own church is an embarrassing rôle; though I have
a horrid feeling that if such mission work is not soon undertaken
the future history of the Church of England is likely to be short.

THE SEEING EYE

The Russians, I am told, report that they have not found God in outer space. On the other hand, a good many people in many different times and countries claim to have found God, or been found by God, here on earth.

The conclusion some want us to draw from these data is that God does not exist. As a corollary, those who think they have met Him on earth were suffering from a delusion.

But other conclusions might be drawn:

1. We have not yet gone far enough in space. There had been ships on the Atlantic for a good time before America was discovered.

2. God does exist but is locally confined to this planet.

3. The Russians did find God in space without knowing it, because they lacked the requisite apparatus for detecting Him.

4. God does exist but is not an object either located in a particular part of space nor diffused, as we once thought 'ether' was, throughout space.

The first two conclusions do not interest me. The sort of religion for which they could be a defence would be a religion for savages: the belief in a local deity who can be contained in a particular temple, island or grove. That, in fact, seems to be the sort of religion about which the Russians—or some Russians, and a good many people in the West—are being irreligious. It is not in the least disquieting that no astronauts have discovered a god of that sort. The really disquieting thing would be if they had.

The third and fourth conclusions are the ones for my money. Looking for God—or Heaven—by exploring space is like reading or seeing all Shakespeare's plays in the hope that you will find Shakespeare as one of the characters or Stratford as one of the places. Shakespeare is in one sense present at every moment in every play. But he is never present in the same way as Falstaff or Lady Macbeth. Nor is he diffused through the play like a gas.

If there were an idiot who thought plays existed on their own, without an author (not to mention actors, producer, manager, stagehands and what not), our belief in Shakespeare would not be much affected by his saying, quite truly, that he had studied all the plays and never found Shakespeare in them.

The rest of us, in varying degrees according to our perceptiveness, 'found Shakespeare' in the plays. But it is a quite different sort of 'finding' from anything our poor friend has in mind.

Even he has in reality been in some way affected by Shakespeare, but without knowing it. He lacked the necessary apparatus for detecting Shakespeare.

Now of course this is only an analogy. I am not suggesting at all that the existence of God is as easily established as the existence of Shakespeare. My point is that, if God does exist, He is related to the universe more as an author is related to a play than as one object in the universe is related to another.

If God created the universe, He created space-time, which is to the universe as the metre is to a poem or the key is to music. To look for Him as one item within the framework which He Himself invented is nonsensical.

If God—such a God as any adult religion believes in—exists, mere movement in space will never bring you any nearer to Him or any farther from Him than you are at this very moment. You can neither reach Him nor avoid Him by travelling to Alpha Centauri or even to other galaxies. A fish is no more, and no less, in the sea after it has swum a thousand miles than it was when it set out.

How, then, it may be asked, can we either reach or avoid Him?

The avoiding, in many times and places, has proved so difficult that a very large part of the human race failed to achieve it. But in our own time and place it is extremely easy. Avoid silence, avoid solitude, avoid any train of thought that leads off the beaten track. Concentrate on money, sex, status, health and (above all) on your own grievances. Keep the radio on. Live in a crowd. Use plenty of sedation. If you must read books, select them very carefully. But you'd be safer to stick to the papers. You'll find the advertisements helpful; especially those with a sexy or a snobbish appeal.

About the reaching. I am a far less reliable guide. That is because I never had the experience of looking for God. It was the other way round; He was the hunter (or so it seemed to me) and I was the deer. He stalked me like a redskin, took unerring aim, and fired. And I am very thankful that that is how the first (conscious) meeting occurred. It forearms one against subsequent fears that the whole thing was only wish fulfilment. Something one didn't wish for can hardly be that.

But it is significant that this long-evaded encounter happened at a time when I was making a serious effort to obey my conscience. No doubt it was far less serious than I supposed, but it was the most serious I had made for a long time.

One of the first results of such an effort is to bring your picture of yourself down to something nearer life-size. And presently you begin to wonder whether you are yet, in any full sense, a person at all; whether you are entitled to call yourself 'I' (it is a sacred name). In that way, the process is like being psycho-analysed, only cheaper—I mean, in dollars; in some other ways it may be more costly. You find that what you called yourself is only a thin film on the surface of an unsounded and dangerous sea. But not merely dangerous. Radiant things, delights and inspirations, come to the surface as well as snarling resentments and nagging lusts.

One's ordinary self is, then, a mere façade. There's a huge area out of sight behind it.

And then, if one listens to the physicists, one discovers that the same is true of all the things around us. These tables and chairs, this magazine, the trees, clouds and mountains are façades. Poke (scientifically) into them and you find the unimaginable structure of the atom. That is, in the long run, you find mathematical formulas.

There are you (whatever YOU means) sitting reading. Out there (whatever THERE means) is a white page with black marks on it. And both are façades. Behind both lies—well, Whatever-it-is. The psychologists, and the theologians, though they use different symbols, equally use symbols when they try to probe the depth behind the façade called YOU. That is, they can't really say 'It is this', but they can say 'It is in some way like this.' And the physicists, trying to probe behind the other façade, can give you only mathematics. And the mathematics may be true about the reality, but it can hardly be the reality itself, any more than contour lines are real mountains.

I am not in the least blaming either set of experts for this state of affairs. They make progress. They are always discovering things. If governments make a bad use of the physicists' discoveries, or if novelists and biographers make a bad use of the psychologists' discoveries, the experts are not to blame. The point, however, is that every fresh discovery, far from dissipating, deepens the mystery.

Presently, if you are a person of a certain sort, if you are one who has to believe that all things which exist must have unity it will seem to you irresistibly probable that what lies ultimately behind the one façade also lies ultimately behind the other. And then—again, if you are that sort of person—you may come to be convinced that your contact with that mystery in the area you call yourself is a good deal closer than your contact through what you call matter. For in the one case I, the ordinary, conscious I, am continuous with the unknown depth.

And after that, you may come (some do) to believe that that voice—like all the rest, I must speak symbolically—that voice which speaks is your conscience and in some of your intensest joys, which is sometimes so obstinately silent, sometimes so easily silenced, and then at other times so loud and emphatic, is in fact the closest contact you have with the mystery; and therefore finally to be trusted, obeyed, feared and desired more than all other things. But still, if you are a different sort of person, you will not come to this conclusion.

I hope everyone sees how this is related to the astronautical question from which we started. The process I have been sketching may equally well occur, or fail to occur, wherever you happen to be. I don't mean that all religious and all irreligious people have either taken this step or refused to take it. Once religion and its opposite are in the world—and they have both been in it for a very long time—the majority in both camps will be simply conformists. Their belief or disbelief will result from their upbringing and from the prevailing tone of the circles they live in. They will have done no hunting for God and no flying for God on their own. But if no minorities who did these things on their own existed I presume that the conforming majorities would not exist either. (Don't imagine I'm despising these majorities. I am sure the one contains better Christians than I am; the other, nobler atheists than I was.)

Space-travel really has nothing to do with the matter. To some, God is discoverable everywhere; to others, nowhere. Those who do not find Him on earth are unlikely to find Him in space. (Hang it all, we're in space already; every year we go a huge circular tour in space.) But send a saint up in a spaceship and he'll find God in space as he found God on earth. Much depends on the seeing eye.

And this is especially confirmed by my own religion, which is Christianity. When I said a while ago that it was nonsensical to look for God as one item within His own work, the universe, some readers may have wanted to protest. They wanted to say, 'But surely, according to Christianity, that is just what did once happen? Surely the central doctrine is that God became man and walked about among other men in Palestine? If that is not appearing as an item in His own work, what is it?'

The objection is much to the point. To meet it, I must readjust my old analogy of the play. One might imagine a play in which the dramatist introduced himself as a character into his own play and was pelted off the stage as an impudent impostor by the other characters. It might be rather a good play; if I had any talent for the theatre I'd try my hand at writing it. But since (as far as I know) such a play doesn't exist, we had better change to a narrative work; a story into which the author puts himself as one of the characters.

We have a real instance of this in Dante's *Divine Comedy*. Dante is (1) the muse outside the poem who is inventing the whole thing, and (2) a character inside the poem, whom the other characters meet and with whom they hold conversations. Where the analogy breaks down is that everything the poem contains is merely imaginary, in that the characters have no free will. They (the characters) can say to Dante only what Dante (the poet) has decided to put into their mouths. I do not think we humans are related to God in that way. I think God can make things which not only—like a poet's or novelist's characters—*seem* to have a partially independent life, but really have it. But the analogy furnishes a crude model of the Incarnation in two respects: (1) Dante the poet and Dante the character are in a sense one, but in another sense two. This is a faint and far-off suggestion of what theologians mean by the 'union of the two natures' (divine and human) in Christ. (2) The other people in the poem meet and see and hear Dante; but they have not even the faintest suspicion that he is making the whole world in which they exist and has a life of his own, outside it, independent of it.

It is the second point which is most relevant. For the Christian story is that Christ was perceived to be God by very few people indeed; perhaps, for a time only by St Peter, who would also, and for the same reason, have found God in space. For Christ said to Peter, 'Flesh and blood have not taught you this.' The methods of science do not discover facts of that order.

Indeed the expectation of finding God by astronautics would be very like trying to verify or falsify the divinity of Christ by taking specimens of His blood or dissecting Him. And in their own way they did both. But they were no wiser than before. What is required is a certain faculty of recognition.

If you do not at all know God, of course you will not recognize Him, either in Jesus or in outer space.

The fact that we have not found God in space does not, then, bother me in the least. Nor am I much concerned about the 'space race' between America and Russia. The more money, time, skill and zeal they both spend on that rivalry, the less, we may hope they will have to spend on armaments. Great powers might be more usefully, but are seldom less dangerously, employed than in fabricating costly objects and flinging them, as you might say, overboard. Good luck to it! It is an excellent way of letting off steam.

But there are three ways in which space-travel will bother me if it reaches the stage for which most people are hoping.

The first is merely sentimental, or perhaps aesthetic. No moonlit night will ever be the same to me again if, as I look up at that pale disc, I must think 'Yes: up there to the left is the Russian area, and over there to the right is the American bit. And up at the top is the place which is now threatening to produce a crisis.' The immemorial Moon—the Moon of the myths, the poets, the lovers—will have been taken from us forever. Part of our mind, a huge mass of our emotional wealth, will have gone. Artemis, Diana, the silver planet belonged in that fashion to all humanity: he who first reaches it steals something from us all.

Secondly, a more practical issue will arise when, if ever, we discover rational creatures on other planets. I think myself, this is a very remote contingency. The balance of probability is against life on any other planet of the solar system. We shall hardly find it nearer than the stars. And even if we reach the Moon we shall be no nearer to stellar travel than the first man who paddled across a river was to crossing the Pacific.

This thought is welcome to me because, to be frank, I have no pleasure in looking forward to a meeting between humanity and any alien rational species. I observe how the white man has hitherto treated the black, and how, even among civilized men, the stronger have treated the weaker. If we encounter in the depth of space a race, however innocent and amiable, which is technologically weaker than ourselves, I do not doubt that the same revolting story will be repeated. We shall enslave, deceive, exploit or exterminate; at the very least we shall corrupt it with our vices and infect it with our diseases.

We are not fit yet to visit other worlds. We have filled our own with massacre, torture, syphilis, famine, dust bowls and with all that is hideous to ear or eye. Must we go on to infect new realms?

Of course we might find a species stronger than ourselves. In that case we shall have met, if not God, at least God's judgement in space. But once more the detecting apparatus will be inadequate. We shall think it just our bad luck if righteous creatures rightly destroy those who come to reduce them to misery.

It was in part these reflections that first moved me to make my own small contributions to science fiction. In those days writers in that genre almost automatically represented the inhabitants of other worlds as monsters and the terrestrial invaders as good. Since then the opposite set-up has become fairly common. If I could believe that I had in any degree contributed to this change, I should be a proud man.[1]

The same problem, by the way, is beginning to threaten us as regards the dolphins. I don't think it has yet been proved that they are rational. But if they are, we have no more right to enslave them than to enslave our fellow-men. And some of us will continue to say this, but we shall be mocked.

The third thing is this. Some people are troubled, and others are delighted, at the idea of finding not one, but perhaps innumerable rational species scattered about the universe. In both cases the emotion arises from a belief that such discoveries would be fatal to Christian theology. For it will be said that theology connects the Incarnation of God with the Fall and Redemption of man. And this would seem to attribute to our species and to our little planet a central position in cosmic history which is not credible if rationally inhabited planets are to be had by the million.

Older readers will, with me, notice the vast change in astronomical speculation which this view involves. When we were boys all astronomers, so far as I know, impressed upon us the antecedent improbabilities of life in any part of the universe whatever. It was not thought unlikely that this earth was the solitary exception to a universal reign of the inorganic. Now Professor Hoyle, and many with him, say that in so vast a universe life must have occurred in times and places without number. The interesting thing is that I have heard both these estimates used as arguments against Christianity.

Now it seems to me that we must find out more than we can at present know—which is nothing—about hypothetical rational species before we can say what theological corollaries or difficulties their discovery would raise.

We might, for example, find a race which was, like us, rational but, unlike us, innocent—no wars nor any other wickedness among them; all peace and good fellowship. I don't think any

[1 The reference is to Lewis's interplanetary novels, *Out of the Silent Planet*, *Perelandra* and *That Hideous Strength*. He was probably the first writer to introduce the idea of having *fallen* terrestrial invaders discover on other planets—in his own books, Mars (*Out of the Silent Planet*) and Venus (*Perelandra*)—*unfallen* rational beings who were in no need of redemption and with nothing to learn from us. See also his essay, 'Will We Lose God in Outer Space?' *Christian Herald*, vol. LXXXI (April, 1958), pp. 19, 74-6.]

Christian would be puzzled to find that they knew no story of an Incarnation or Redemption, and might even find our story hard to understand or accept if we told it to them. There would have been no Redemption in such a world because it would not have needed redeeming. 'They that are whole need not the physician.' The sheep that has never strayed need not be sought for. We should have much to learn from such people and nothing to teach them. If we were wise, we should fall at their feet. But probably we should be unable to 'take it'. We'd find some reason for exterminating them.

Again, we might find a race which, like ours, contained both good and bad. And we might find that for them, as for us, something had been done: that at some point in their history some great interference for the better, believed by some of them to be supernatural, had been recorded, and that its effects, though often impeded and perverted, were still alive among them. It need not, as far as I can see, have conformed to the pattern of Incarnation, Passion, Death and Resurrection. God may have other ways—how should I be able to imagine them?—of redeeming a lost world. And Redemption in that alien mode might not be easily recognizable by our missionaries, let alone by our atheists.

We might meet a species which, like us, needed Redemption but had not been given it. But would this fundamentally be more of a difficulty than any Christian's first meeting with a new tribe of savages? It would be our duty to preach the Gospel to them. For if they are rational, capable both of sin and repentance, they are our brethren, whatever they look like. Would this spreading of the Gospel from earth, through man, imply a pre-eminence for earth and man? Not in any real sense. If a thing is to begin at all, it must begin at some particular time and place; and any time and place raises the question: 'Why just then and just there?' One can conceive an extraterrestrial development of Christianity so brilliant that earth's place in the story might sink to that of a prologue.

Finally, we might find a race which was strictly diabolical—no tiniest spark felt in them from which any goodness could ever be coaxed into the feeblest glow; all of them incurably perverted through and through. What then? We Christians had always been told that there were creatures like that in existence. True, we thought they were all incorporeal spirits. A minor readjustment thus becomes necessary.

But all this is in the realm of fantastic speculation. We are trying to cross a bridge, not only before we come to it, but even before we know there is a river that needs bridging.